# knitted fairy tales

# knitted
# fairy tales

Recreate the famous stories with knitted toys

Sarah Keen

THE GUILD OF MASTER CRAFTSMAN PUBLICATIONS

# Dedicated
# to Harry

First published 2014 by
Guild of Master Craftsman Publications Ltd
Castle Place, 166 High Street, Lewes,
East Sussex BN7 1XU

Text and designs © Sarah Keen, 2014
Copyright in the Work © GMC Publications Ltd,
2014

ISBN 978 1 86108 969 4

A catalogue record for this book is available
from the British Library.

Publisher  Jonathan Bailey
Production Manager  Jim Bulley
Managing Editor  Gerrie Purcell
Senior Project Editor  Dominique Page
Editor  Lorraine Slipper
Pattern Checker  Marilyn Wilson
Managing Art Editor  Gilda Pacitti
Designer  Ginny Zeal
Photographer  Andrew Perris
Illustrators  Rebecca Mothersole
and Simon Rodway

Set in Frutiger
Colour origination by GMC Reprographics
Printed and bound in China

# Where to find the fairy tales

# Introduction

Designing and creating the projects for this book has been an exciting time for me, and they follow on nicely from my previous title, *Knitted Nursery Rhymes*. The characters you will find here appear in enchanting fairy tales, such as *Snow White*, *Cinderella* and *Sleeping Beauty*, and other popular tales that children enjoy. Having the toys to act out the story will delight any child... and they all lived happily ever after!

I've had great fun putting together these designs and hope you too will find enjoyment in whichever toys you decide to make.

*Sarah Keen*

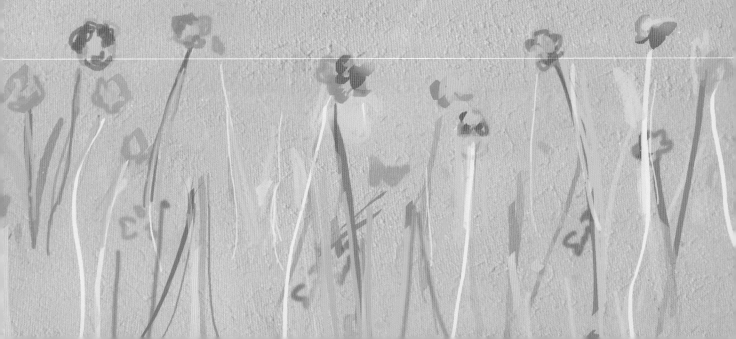

"I shall make your fortune for you."

"I'd give up my life in the sea if I could be with my prince."

"Who will help me
plant these seeds?"

They tried the glass slipper
on Cinderella and it fitted
her perfectly.

"Why Grandma, what big eyes you have!"

LITTLE RED RIDING HOOD >> 118

"Heigh-ho, heigh-ho,
it's off to work we go..."

The bears came home to find
someone had been eating
their porridge!

The prince awoke
her with a kiss.

"I want to be
a real boy."

"I'll huff, and I'll puff, and I'll blow your house down!"

THREE LITTLE PIGS >> 94

Deep in the forest, they
found a cottage made from
gingerbread, sweets and icing.

The princess would do anything to get back her golden ball – even kiss a frog!

154 << THE GINGERBREAD MAN

"Run, run, as fast as you can! You can't catch me, I'm the Gingerbread Man!"

"I wonder if she is a real princess?"

Overnight, an enormous
beanstalk had grown
outside Jack's window.

One day, a long, long time ago, a carpenter was carving a puppet out of wood when all of a sudden the puppet shouted: "Ouch! That hurt!" The carpenter couldn't believe it – the wooden puppet was alive! He called the puppet Pinocchio...

# PINOCCHIO

# Information you'll need

### Finished size
Pinocchio measures 12in (30cm) high

### Materials
**Any DK (US: light worsted) yarn**
**Note:** amounts are approximate
25g fawn (A)
5g white (B)
5g yellow (C)
5g black (D)
5g medium brown (E)
5g dark brown (F)
5g blue (G)
10g red (H)
Oddments of black and red for embroidery
1 pair of 3.25mm (UK10:US3) needles
Knitters' blunt-ended pins and a needle for sewing up
Tweezers for stuffing small parts (optional)
Acrylic toy stuffing

### Tension
26 sts x 34 rows measure 4in (10cm) square over st-st using 3.25mm needles and DK yarn before stuffing.

### Working instructions
Sew up all row-end seams on right side using mattress stitch, unless otherwise stated; a one-stitch seam allowance has been allowed for this.

# How to make Pinocchio

## Body and head

Beg at lower edge of body, using the thumb method and A, cast on 28 sts, WS facing to beg.

Place a marker at centre of cast-on edge.

**Rows 1 to 11:** Beg with a p row, work 11 rows in st-st.

**Rows 12 to 23:** Change to B for upper body and work 12 rows in st-st.

**Row 24:** K5, (k2tog) twice, k10, (k2tog) twice, k5 (24 sts).

**Rows 25 to 27:** Beg with a p row, work 3 rows in st-st.

**Rows 28 and 29:** Change to A for head and work 2 rows in st-st.

**Row 30:** K1, (m1, k2) to last st, m1, k1 (36 sts).

**Rows 31 to 49:** Beg with a p row, work 19 rows in st-st.

### Shape top of head

**Row 50:** (K2tog, k2) to end (27 sts).

**Row 51 and foll alt row:** Purl.

**Row 52:** (K2tog, k1) to end (18 sts).

**Row 54:** (K2tog) to end (9 sts).

Thread yarn through sts on needle, pull tight and secure by threading yarn a second time through sts.

## Legs (make 2)

Beg at lower edge using the thumb method and A, cast on 14 sts, WS facing to beg.

**Rows 1 to 15:** Beg with a p row, work 15 rows in st-st.

### Work joint

**Rows 16 to 19:** Beg with a p row, work 4 rows in rev st-st.

**Rows 20 and 21:** K 1 row then p 1 row.

### Shape upper leg

**Row 22:** K1, m1, k4, (k2tog) twice, k4, m1, k1 (14 sts).

**Rows 23 to 25:** Beg with a p row, work 3 rows in st-st.

**Rows 26 to 33:** Rep rows 22 to 25 twice more.

**Row 34:** As row 22.

**Row 35:** Purl.

Cast off.

## Shorts and belt

### First leg

Beg at lower edge using the thumb method and C, cast on 20 sts.

**Row 1 (RS):** Purl.

**Rows 2 to 8:** Beg with a p row, work 7 rows in st-st.

**Row 9:** K1, m1, k to last st, m1, k1 (22 sts).

**Row 10:** Purl.

**Rows 11 and 12:** Rep rows 9 and 10 once (24 sts).

Break yarn and set aside.

### Second leg

Work as first leg but do not break yarn.

### Join legs

**Row 13:** K across sts of second leg and then, with the same yarn, cont k across sts of first leg (48 sts).

Place a marker on first and last st of the last row.

**Rows 14 to 16:** Beg with a p row, work 3 rows in st-st.

**Row 17:** *K5, (k2tog, k2) 4 times, k3; rep from * once (40 sts).

**Rows 18 to 22:** Beg with a p row, work 5 rows in st-st.

Change to D for belt and dec:

**Row 23:** (K7, k2tog, k2, k2tog, k7) twice (36 sts).

**Row 24:** Knit.

**Rows 25 to 27:** Beg with a k row, work 3 rows in st-st, ending with a RS row.

Cast off kwise.

## Shoes (make 2)

Beg at heel using the thumb method and E, cast on 6 sts.

**Row 1 (WS):** Purl.
**Row 2:** (K1, m1) twice, k2, (m1, k1) twice (10 sts).
**Row 3:** Purl.
**Row 4:** (K1, m1) 4 times, k2, (m1, k1) 4 times (18 sts).
**Rows 5 to 9:** Beg with a p row, work 5 rows in st-st.
**Row 10:** K8, m1, k2, m1, k8 (20 sts).
**Rows 11 to 17:** Beg with a p row, work 7 rows in st-st.
**Row 18:** (K2tog) to end (10 sts).
**Row 19:** Purl.
**Row 20:** (K2tog) to end (5 sts).
Thread yarn through sts on needle, pull tight and secure by threading yarn a second time through sts.

## Arms and hands (make 2)
Beg at shoulder using the thumb method and B, cast on 4 sts.
**Row 1 (WS):** Purl.
**Row 2:** K1, m1, k to last st, m1 k1 (6 sts).
**Rows 3 to 8:** Rep rows 1 and 2, 3 times more (12 sts).
Place a marker on first and last st of the last row.
**Rows 9 to 13:** Beg with a p row work 5 rows in st-st.
**Work cuff**
**Rows 14 and 15:** P 1 row then k 1 row.
**Rows 16 to 19:** Change to A and beg with a k row, work 4 rows in st-st.
**Work joint**
**Rows 20 and 21:** P 1 row then k 1 row.
**Rows 22 to 29:** Beg with a k row, work 8 rows in st-st.
**Row 30:** K5, k2tog, k5 (11 sts).
**Row 31 and foll 2 alt rows:** Purl.
**Row 32:** K5, m1, k1, m1, k5 (13 sts).
**Row 34:** K5, m1, k3, m1, k5 (15 sts).
**Row 36:** K5, m1, k5, m1, k5 (17 sts).
**Row 37:** P11, turn.

**Row 38:** K5, turn, break yarn and thread through these 5 sts, pull tight and secure by threading yarn a second time through sts then oversew row ends of thumb on RS. With WS facing, rejoin yarn to rem sts half way along row and p to end.
**Rows 39 and 40:** Push rem sts tog and work 2 rows in st-st (12 sts).
**Row 41:** (K2tog) to end (6 sts).
Thread yarn through sts on needle, pull tight and secure by threading yarn a second time through sts.

## Nose
Beg at tip using the thumb method and A, cast on 6 sts, WS facing to beg.
**Rows 1 to 3:** Beg with a p row, work 3 rows in st-st.
**Row 4:** K2, (m1, k2) twice (8 sts).
**Row 5:** Purl.
Cast off.

## Hair
Beg at lower edge using the thumb method and F, cast on 36 sts and work in g-st, RS facing to beg.
**Rows 1 to 18:** Work 18 rows in g-st.
**Shape crown**
**Row 19:** (K2tog, k2) to end (27 sts).
**Row 20 and foll alt row:** Knit.
**Row 21:** (K2tog, k1) to end (18 sts).
**Row 23:** (K2tog) to end (9 sts).
Thread yarn through sts on needle, pull tight and secure by threading yarn a second time through sts.

## Hat
Beg at brim using the thumb method and G, cast on 48 sts and beg in g-st, RS facing to beg.
**Rows 1 to 10:** Work 10 rows in g-st.
**Rows 11 and 12:** Change to H and k 1 row then p 1 row.
**Row 13:** (K2tog, k4) to end (40 sts).
**Rows 14 to 18:** Beg with a p row, work 5 rows in st-st.
**Row 19:** (K2tog, k3) to end (32 sts).
**Rows 20 to 22:** Beg with a p row, work 3 rows in st-st.
**Row 23:** (K2tog, k2) to end (24 sts).
**Row 24:** Purl.
**Row 25:** (K2tog, k1) to end (16 sts).
**Row 26:** (P2tog) to end (8 sts).
Thread yarn through sts on needle, pull tight and secure by threading yarn a second time through sts.

## Waistcoat

Beg at lower edge using the thumb method and H, cast on 36 sts and work in g-st, RS facing to beg.

**Rows 1 to 6:** Work 6 rows in g-st.
**Row 7:** K6, k2tog, k20, k2tog, k6 (34 sts).
**Rows 8 to 10:** Work 3 rows in g-st.
**Row 11:** K6, k2tog, k18, k2tog, k6 (32 sts).
**Rows 12 to 15:** Work 4 rows in g-st, ending with a RS row.
**Row 16:** K6, cast off 2 sts (7 sts now on RH needle), k15, cast off 2 sts, k5 (28 sts).
**Row 17:** K6, turn and work on these 6 sts.
**Rows 18 to 20:** Work 3 rows in g-st.
**Row 21:** K1, k2tog, k to end (5 sts).
**Rows 22 to 24:** Work 3 rows in g-st.

**Row 25:** K1, k2tog, k2 (4 sts).
**Rows 26 to 31:** Work 6 rows in g-st, ending with a RS row.
Cast off in g-st.
**Row 32:** Rejoin yarn to rem sts and k16, turn and work on these 16 sts.
**Rows 33 to 48:** Work 16 rows in g-st, ending with RS row.
Cast off in g-st.
**Row 49:** Rejoin yarn to rem sts and k6.
**Rows 50 to 52:** Work 3 rows in g-st.
**Row 53:** K3, k2tog, k1 (5 sts).
**Rows 54 to 56:** Work 3 rows in g-st.
**Row 57:** K2, k2tog, k1 (4 sts).
**Rows 58 to 63:** Work 6 rows in g-st, ending with a RS row.
Cast off in g-st.

## Bow tie

Using the thumb method and G, cast on 6 sts and work in g-st, RS facing to beg.
**Rows 1 to 5:** Work 5 rows in g-st.
Cast off in g-st.

# Making up

### Body and head

Sew up row ends of body and head and stuff. Bring marker and seam together at lower edge and oversew lower edge. To shape neck, take a double length of white yarn and sew a running stitch around last row of upper body, sewing in and out of every half stitch. Pull tight and knot yarn and sew ends into neck.

## Legs

Sew up row ends of legs and with this seam at one side, sew across the middle of joint. Stuff legs at both ends, pushing stuffing in with tweezers or tip of scissors. With leg seam at inside edge, oversew cast-off stitches, and sew cast-off stitches of legs to lower edge of body.

## Shorts and belt

Sew up leg seams of shorts from lower edge to markers at crotch. Sew round crotch by oversewing and sew up row ends of shorts and belt at centre back. Place shorts on doll and sew cast-off stitches of belt to first row of upper body all the way round.

## Shoes

Gather round cast-on stitches of each shoe, pull tight and secure. Sew up row ends of shoes leaving a gap, stuff and sew up gap. With seam at centre of underneath, pin and sew shoes to lower edge of legs.

## Arms and hands

Sew up row ends of hands and stuff hands and thumb, pushing stuffing in with tweezers or tip of scissors. Sew up arms from wrist to joint and stuff lower arms. With seam at one side, sew across middle of joint. Continue sewing up row ends of arms to markers at underarm and stuff top of arms, pushing stuffing in with tweezers or tip of scissors. Leaving armholes open, sew arms to doll.

## Nose and features

Mark position of eyes with two pins on 12th row above neck with four clear knitted stitches in between. Begin and fasten off features at top of head under hair and embroider eyes in black, making a ring of five chain stitches around pins and join ring with a chain stitch. Using picture as a guide, embroider eyebrows with straight stitches. Sew up row ends of nose and sew base of nose to the 8th to 10th rows above neck at centre front. Embroider mouth in red over six stitches on the 4th to 6th rows above neck, making a shallow 'v' shape.

## Hair

Oversew row ends of hair and place on doll and, with seam at centre back, pull hair down to ¾in (2cm) above neck at back. Sew lower edge of hair to head using back stitch all the way round.

## Hat

Fold brim under and sew in place. Sew up row ends of hat from top of hat to brim and oversew row ends of brim. Lightly stuff top of hat and pin and sew hat to head using back stitch on right side of base of brim, sewing through hat to head.

## Waistcoat

Oversew shoulders of waistcoat and place on doll. Sew back of waistcoat to neck at back.

## Bow tie

To shape bow tie, wind matching yarn around middle of bow tie a few times and tie ends at back. Sew bow tie to centre front of neck.

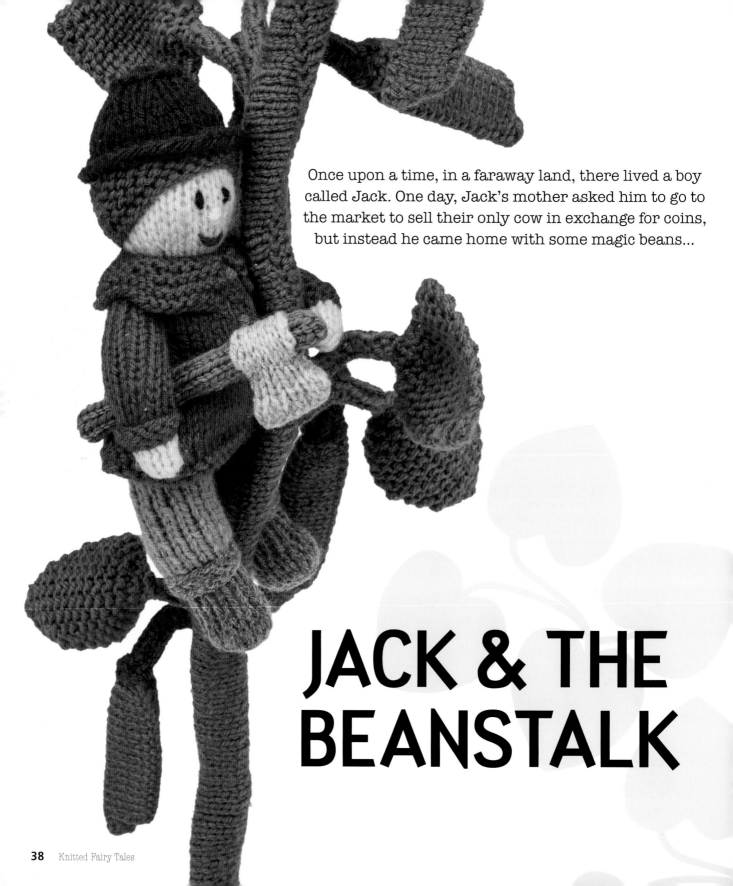

Once upon a time, in a faraway land, there lived a boy called Jack. One day, Jack's mother asked him to go to the market to sell their only cow in exchange for coins, but instead he came home with some magic beans...

# JACK & THE BEANSTALK

# Information you'll need

## Finished sizes

Jack measures 7½in (19cm) high

Jack's Mother measures 8½in (22cm) high

Cow measures 5¼in (13cm) high

Strange Little Man measures 5½in (14cm) high

Beans measure 1in (2.5cm) across

Beanstalk measures 34in (85cm) high

Giant measures 16in (40.5cm) high

Hen, Golden Eggs and Nest measure 2¼in (6cm) high

Harp measures 4½in (11cm) high

Axe measures 3½in (9cm) long

## Materials

### Any DK (US: light worsted) yarn

**Note:** amounts are approximate

5g dark grey (A)

30g white (B)

10g rust (C)

30g pale pink (D)

5g khaki green (E)

10g pale brown (F)

10g medium brown (G)

5g purple (H)

15g petrol blue (I)

5g pale blue (J)

30g dark brown (K)

10g red (L)

10g black (M)

5g golden cream (N)

5g dark green (O)

5g lilac (P)

5g gold (Q)

5g lime green (R)

5g duck egg blue (S)

5g butter milk (T)

100g leaf green (U)

20g apple green (V)

20g mustard (W)

5g silver grey (X)

Oddments of black, red, dark grey, pale pink, rust and gold for embroidery

1 pair of 3.25mm (UK10:US3) needles and a spare needle of the same size

A 3.25mm (US3) circular needle

Knitters' blunt-ended pins and a needle for sewing up

Tweezers for stuffing small parts (optional)

Acrylic toy stuffing

15 chenille sticks

3 drinking straws

Red pencil for shading cheeks

## Tension

26 sts x 34 rows measure 4in (10cm) square over st-st using 3.25mm needles and DK yarn before stuffing.

## Working instructions

Sew up all row-end seams on right side using mattress stitch, unless otherwise stated; a one-stitch seam allowance has been allowed for this.

39

# How to make Jack

## Boots, legs, body and head
### Right leg
Beg at sole of boot, using the thumb method and A, cast on 10 sts.
Place a marker on cast-on edge between the 4th and 5th st of the sts just cast on.
**Row 1 (WS):** Purl.
**Row 2:** K1, (m1, k1) to end (19 sts).
**Rows 3 to 5:** Beg with a p row, work 3 rows in st-st.
### Shape boot
**Row 6:** K1, (k2tog) 7 times, k4 (12 sts).
**Rows 7 to 27:** Beg with a p row, work 21 rows in st-st.
Break yarn and set aside.
### Left leg
Beg at sole of boot, using the thumb method and A, cast on 10 sts.
Place a marker on cast-on edge between the 6th and 7th st of the sts just cast on.
**Row 1 (WS):** Purl.
**Row 2:** K1, (m1, k1) to end (19 sts).
**Rows 3 to 5:** Beg with a p row, work 3 rows in st-st.
### Shape boot
**Row 6:** K4, (k2tog) 7 times, k1 (12 sts).
**Rows 7 to 27:** Beg with a p row, work 21 rows in st-st.
### Join legs
**Row 28:** Change to B for lower body and k across sts of left leg and then with the same yarn, cont k across sts of right leg (24 sts).
**Rows 29 to 35:** Beg with a p row, work 7 rows in st-st.
**Rows 36 to 49:** Change to C for upper body and work 14 rows in st-st.
**Rows 50 and 51:** Change to D for head and work 2 rows in st-st.
**Row 52:** K3, (m1, k6) 3 times, m1, k3 (28 sts).
**Rows 53 to 59:** Beg with a p row, work 7 rows in st-st.

## Shape top of head
**Row 60:** (K2tog, k2) to end (21 sts).
**Row 61 and foll alt row:** Purl.
**Row 62:** (K2tog, k1) to end (14 sts).
**Row 64:** (K2tog) to end (7 sts).
Thread yarn through sts on needle and leave loose.

## Breeches
### First leg
Beg at lower edge, using the thumb method and E, cast on 18 sts, RS facing to beg.
**Rows 1 to 12:** Beg with a k row, work 12 rows in st-st.
**Rows 13 and 14:** Work 2 rows in st-st and cast off 1 st at beg of each of these 2 rows (16 sts).
Break yarn and set aside.

## Second leg

Work as first leg but do not break yarn.

**Join legs**

**Row 15:** With RS facing, k across sts of second leg, and then with the same yarn cont k across sts of first leg (32 sts).

**Rows 16 to 22:** Beg with a p row, work 7 rows in st-st.

Cast off.

## Boot tops (make 2)

Using the thumb method and A, cast on 18 sts, RS facing to beg.

Cast off pwise.

## Coat

Beg at lower edge, using the thumb method and C, cast on 46 sts and beg in g-st, RS facing to beg.

**Rows 1 and 2:** Work 2 rows in g-st.

**Rows 3 to 10:** Beg with a k row, work 8 rows in st-st and k the first st and last st on every p row.

**Row 11:** K4, (k2tog, k2) to last 2 sts, k2 (36 sts).

**Rows 12 to 22:** Beg with a p row, work 11 rows in st-st and k the first st and last st on every p row.

**Row 23:** K3, (k2tog) 6 times, k6, (k2tog) 6 times, k3 (24 sts).

Cast off pwise.

## Sleeves and hands (make 2)

Beg at shoulder, using the thumb method and C, cast on 4 sts.

**Row 1 (WS):** Purl.

**Row 2:** K1, m1, k to last st, m1, k1 (6 sts).

**Rows 3 to 8:** Rep rows 1 and 2, 3 times more (12 sts).

Place a marker on first and last st of the last row.

**Rows 9 to 17:** Beg with a p row, work 9 rows in st-st.

**Row 18:** K1, k2tog, (k2, k2tog) twice, k1 (9 sts).

**Rows 19 to 23:** Change to D for hand and beg with a p row, work 5 rows in st-st.

Thread yarn through sts on needle, pull tight and secure by threading yarn a second time through sts.

## Collar

Beg at outside edge, using the thumb method and C, cast on 44 sts and work in g-st, RS facing to beg.

**Rows 1 and 2:** Work 2 rows in g-st.

**Row 3:** *K5, (k2tog) twice, k4, (k2tog) twice, k5; rep from * once (36 sts).

**Row 4 and foll alt row:** Knit.

**Row 5:** *K4, (k2tog) twice, k2, (k2tog) twice, k4; rep from * once (28 sts).

**Row 7:** *K4, k2tog, k2, k2tog, k4; rep from * once (24 sts).

Cast off in g-st.

## Cuffs (make 2)

Using the thumb method and C, cast on 13 sts, RS facing to beg.
Cast off pwise.

## Hair

Beg at lower edge, using the thumb method and F, cast on 28 sts and work in g-st, RS facing to beg.
**Rows 1 to 12:** Work 12 rows in g-st.
**Shape crown**
**Row 13:** (K2tog, k2) to end (21 sts).
**Row 14 and foll alt row:** Knit.
**Row 15:** (K2tog, k1) to end (14 sts).
**Row 17:** (K2tog) to end (7 sts).
Thread yarn through sts on needle, pull tight and secure by threading yarn a second time through sts.

## Hat

Beg at lower edge using the thumb method and G, cast on 40 sts and beg in g-st, RS facing to beg.
**Rows 1 and 2:** Work 2 rows in g-st.
**Row 3:** (K2tog, k3) to end (32 sts).
**Rows 4 to 6:** Beg with a p row, work 3 rows in st-st.
**Row 7:** (K2tog, k2) to end (24 sts).
**Row 8:** Purl.
**Row 9:** (K2tog, k1) to end (16 sts).
**Row 10:** Purl.
**Rows 11 and 12:** P 2 rows for fold line at top of hat.
**Row 13:** (K2tog) to end (8 sts).
Thread yarn through sts on needle, pull tight and secure by threading yarn a second time through sts.

# Making up Jack

## Boots, legs, body and head

Sew up row ends of foot and ankle of boots and, with markers at tips of toes, oversew cast-on stitches; leg seam will be ¼in (6mm) on inside edge of heel. Place a ball of stuffing into toe of each boot, pushing stuffing in with tweezers or tip of scissors. Sew up row ends of legs and sew round crotch. Stuff legs, pushing stuffing in with tweezers or tip of scissors. Sew up row ends of body, up to halfway up head. Stuff body and head and pull stitches on thread tight, fasten off and finish sewing up row ends. To shape neck, take a double length of yarn to match upper body and sew a running stitch round last row of upper body, sewing in and out of every half stitch. Pull tight and knot yarn and sew ends into neck.

## Breeches

Sew up leg seams of breeches from lower edge to crotch. Sew round crotch by oversewing and sew up row ends at centre back. Place breeches on doll, sew cast-off stitches of breeches to first row of upper body all the way round, and sew cast-on stitches of each breeches leg to legs.

## Coat

Place coat around doll and sew up centre front. Sew cast-off stitches of coat to neck all the way round.

## Sleeves and hands

Sew up row ends of hands and place a small ball of stuffing into hands, pushing stuffing in with tweezers or tip of scissors. Sew up sleeves from wrists to markers at underarm. Stuff arms, pushing stuffing in with tweezers or tip of scissors, and leave armholes open. Sew arms to doll at either side, sewing through coat to body.

## Collar

Place collar around neck and sew together under chin. Sew cast-off stitches of collar to neck all the way round.

## Cuffs and boot tops

Place cuffs around wrists and boot tops around top of boots, and oversew row ends. Sew cuffs and boot tops to doll using back stitch down centre all the way round.

## Features

Mark position of eyes with two pins on 6th row above neck with two clear knitted stitches in between. Begin and fasten off features at top of head under hair and embroider eyes in black and work a vertical chain stitch for each eye, starting at marked position and ending on row above. Embroider mouth in red on the 3rd and 4th row below eyes, making a shallow 'v' shape across two stitches. Embroider nose in pale pink at centre front on row below eyes, making a bundle of five horizontal stitches over one stitch. Shade cheeks with a red pencil. Embroider four buttons in dark grey down front of coat making two short horizontal stitches close together for each button (see page 171 for how to begin and fasten off the embroidery invisibly).

## Hair

Oversew row ends of hair and place on doll and, with seam at centre back, pull hair down to neck at back. Sew lower edge of hair to head using back stitch all the way round.

## Hat

Sew up row ends of hat, lightly stuff top of hat and place on head. Pin and sew hat to head using back stitch on right side of base of brim, sewing through hat to head all the way round.

# How to make Jack's Mother

## Shoes, legs, body and head

### Right shoe and leg

Beg at sole of shoe, using the thumb method and H, cast on 14 sts.

Place a marker on cast-on edge between the 5th and 6th st of the sts just cast on.

**Row 1 (WS):** Purl.

**Row 2:** K2, (m1, k2) to end (20 sts).

**Rows 3 to 7:** Beg with a p row, work 5 rows in st-st.

### Shape shoe

**Row 8:** (K1, k2tog) twice, k2, (k2tog, k1) twice, k6 (16 sts).

**Row 9:** Purl.

Change to D for leg and dec:

**Row 10:** (K2, k2tog) twice, k8 (14 sts).

**Rows 11 to 33:** Beg with a p row, work 23 rows in st-st.

Break yarn and set aside.

### Left shoe and leg

Beg at sole of shoe, using the thumb method and H, cast on 14 sts.

Place a marker on cast-on edge between the 9th and 10th st of the sts just cast on.

**Row 1 (WS):** Purl.

**Row 2:** K2, (m1, k2) to end (20 sts).

**Rows 3 to 7:** Beg with a p row, work 5 rows in st-st.

### Shape shoe

**Row 8:** K7, (k2tog, k1) twice, (k1, k2tog) twice, k1 (16 sts).

**Row 9:** Purl.

Change to D for leg and dec:

**Row 10:** K8, (k2tog, k2) twice (14 sts).

**Rows 11 to 33:** Beg with a p row, work 23 rows in st-st.

### Join legs

**Row 34:** Change to B for lower body and k across sts of left leg, and then with the same yarn cont k across sts of right leg (28 sts).

**Rows 35 to 41:** Beg with a p row, work 7 rows in st-st.

**Rows 42 to 51:** Change to I for upper body and work 10 rows in st-st.

**Rows 52 to 55:** Change to D for neck and work 4 rows in st-st.

Place a marker on the last row for neck gathering.

**Rows 56 and 57:** Work 2 rows in st-st.

**Row 58:** *K4, (m1, k2) 4 times, k2; rep from * once (36 sts).

**Rows 59 to 73:** Beg with a p row, work 15 rows in st-st.

### Shape top of head

**Row 74:** (K2tog, k2) to end (27 sts).

**Row 75 and foll alt row:** Purl.

**Row 76:** (K2tog, k1) to end (18 sts).

**Row 78:** (K2tog) to end (9 sts).

Thread yarn through sts on needle and leave loose.

## Skirt of dress

Beg at lower edge of skirt of dress, using the thumb method and I, cast on 72 sts and beg in g-st, RS facing to beg.

**Rows 1 and 2:** Work 2 rows in g-st.

**Rows 3 to 20:** Beg with a k row, work 18 rows in st-st.

**Row 21:** (K2tog, k4) to end (60 sts).

**Rows 22 to 26:** Beg with a p row, work 5 rows in st-st.

**Row 27:** (K2tog, k3) to end (48 sts).

**Rows 28 to 30:** Beg with a p row, work 3 rows in st-st.

Change to B for waistband of apron and dec:

**Row 31:** (K2tog, k2) to end (36 sts).

**Rows 32 and 33:** Work 2 rows in g-st, ending with a RS row.

Cast off in g-st.

## Sleeves and hands (make 2)

Beg at sleeve, using the thumb method and J, cast on 4 sts.

**Row 1 (WS):** Purl.
**Row 2:** K1, (m1, k1) to end (7 sts).
**Row 3:** Purl.
**Row 4:** K1, m1, k to last st, m1, k1 (9 sts).
**Rows 5 to 8:** Rep rows 3 and 4, twice more (13 sts).
Place a marker on first and last st of the last row.
**Rows 9 to 21:** Beg with a p row, work 13 rows in st-st.
**Row 22:** K3, (k2tog, k3) twice (11 sts).
**Rows 23 to 27:** Change to D for hand and beg with a p row, work 5 rows in st-st.
**Row 28:** K2tog, (k1, k2tog) to end (7 sts).
Thread yarn through sts on needle, pull tight and secure by threading yarn a second time through sts.

## Cuffs (make 2)

Using the thumb method and J, cast on 15 sts, RS facing to beg.
Cast off pwise.

## Apron

Beg at lower edge using the thumb method and B, cast on 18 sts and beg in g-st, RS facing to beg.
**Rows 1 and 2:** Work 2 rows in g-st.
**Rows 3 to 12:** Beg with a k row, work 10 rows in st-st and k the first 2 and last 2 sts on every p row.
**Row 13:** K2, (k2tog, k2) to end (14 sts).
**Rows 14 to 18:** Beg with a p row, work 5 rows in st-st and k the first 2 and last 2 sts on every p row.
**Row 19:** K2, (k2tog, k2) to end (11 sts).
Cast off pwise.

## Bow

Using the thumb method and B, cast on 35 sts, RS facing to beg.
Cast off pwise.

## Hair

Beg at lower edge using the thumb method and K, cast on 36 sts and work in g-st, RS facing to beg.
**Rows 1 to 20:** Work 20 rows in g-st.
**Shape crown**
**Row 21:** (K2tog, k2) to end (27 sts).
**Row 22 and foll alt row:** Knit.
**Row 23:** (K2tog, k1) to end (18 sts).
**Row 25:** (K2tog) to end (9 sts).
Thread yarn through sts on needle, pull tight and secure by threading yarn a second time through sts.

## Neckband

Using the thumb method and I, cast on 38 sts, RS facing to beg.
Cast off pwise.

## Headscarf

Using the thumb method and L, cast on 45 sts and work in g-st, RS facing to beg.
**Rows 1 and 2:** Work 2 rows in g-st.
**Row 3:** K2tog, k to last 2 sts, k2tog (43 sts).
**Row 4:** Knit.
**Rows 5 to 28:** Rep rows 3 and 4, 12 times more (19 sts).
**Row 29:** K2tog, k to last 2 sts, k2tog (17 sts).
**Rows 30 to 32:** Work 3 rows in g-st.
**Rows 33 to 56:** Rep rows 29 to 32, 6 times more (5 sts).
**Row 57:** K2tog, k1, k2tog (3 sts).
**Row 58:** K3tog tbl (1 st).
Fasten off.

# Making up Jack's Mother

## Shoes, legs, body and head

Sew up row ends of shoes and, with markers at tips of toes, oversew cast-on stitches; leg seam will be ⅓in (8mm) on inside edge of heel. Sew up ankles and place a ball of stuffing into toes. Sew up row ends of legs and sew round crotch. Stuff legs and sew up body seam. Stuff body and sew up row ends of head to half way up head. Stuff head and pull stitches on a thread tight at top of head, fasten off and finish sewing up row ends. To shape neck, take a double length of yarn in pale pink and sew a running stitch round row with marker, sewing in and out of every half stitch. Pull tight and knot yarn, and sew ends into neck.

## Skirt of dress

Sew up row ends of skirt of dress and, with seam at centre back, place skirt of dress on doll. Sew cast-off stitches at waist to first row of upper body all the way round.

## Sleeves and hands

Sew up row ends of hands and place a small ball of stuffing into hands, pushing stuffing in with tweezers or tip of scissors. Sew up sleeves from wrists to markers at underarm. Stuff sleeves and leave armholes open. Sew arms to doll at either side, sewing cast-on stitches at top of arms to second row below neck.

## Cuffs

Place cuffs around wrists and sew up row ends. Sew cuffs to wrists using back stitch down centre of cuff all the way round.

### Apron

Sew cast-off stitches of apron to waistband of doll at centre front and sew lower edge of apron to skirt.

### Bow

Shape bow into a bow shape and sew to waistband of apron at back.

### Features

Mark position of eyes with two pins on 9th row above neck with three clear knitted stitches in between. Begin and fasten off features at top of head under hair and embroider eyes with a double length of black yarn by working a vertical chain stitch for each eye, starting at marked position and ending on second row above marked position. Embroider mouth in red on the 4th and 5th rows below eyes, making a shallow 'v' shape across two stitches. Embroider nose in pale pink at centre front on row below eyes, making a bundle of five horizontal stitches over one stitch. Shade cheeks with a red pencil.

### Hair

Oversew row ends of hair and place on doll and, with seam at centre back, pull hair down to neck at back. Sew lower edge of hair to head using back stitch all the way round.

### Neckband

Place neckband around neck and oversew row ends. Pin and sew neckband around top of dress and over shoulders using back stitch down centre of band.

### Headscarf

Place headscarf around head and join row ends of cast-on stitches at back. Sew lower edge in place around head and fold point of headscarf down at back and sew in place.

## How to make Cow

### Body

Beg at lower edge, using the thumb method and B, cast on 32 sts, WS facing to beg.

**Row 1 and foll 2 alt rows:** Purl.
**Row 2:** (K1, m1, k1, m1, k12, m1, k1, m1, k1) twice (40 sts).
**Row 4:** (K1, m1, k2, m1, k14, m1, k2, m1, k1) twice (48 sts).
**Row 6:** (K1, m1, k3, m1, k16, m1, k3, m1, k1) twice (56 sts).
**Rows 7 to 25:** Beg with a p row, work 19 rows in st-st.
**Row 26:** (K2tog) twice, k20, (k2tog) 4 times, k20, (k2tog) twice (48 sts).
**Row 27 and foll alt row:** Purl.
**Row 28:** (K2tog) twice, k16, (k2tog) 4 times, k16, (k2tog) twice (40 sts).
**Row 30:** (K2tog) twice, k12, (k2tog) 4 times, k12, (k2tog) twice (32 sts).
Cast off pwise.

### Legs (make 4)

Beg at top edge, using the thumb method and B, cast on 19 sts.
**Row 1 (WS):** P12, turn.
**Row 2:** S1k, k4, turn.
**Row 3:** S1p, p to end.
**Rows 4 to 11:** Work 8 rows in st-st.
**Rows 12 to 15:** Change to M and work 4 rows in st-st.
**Row 16:** K1, (k2tog, k1) to end (13 sts).
Cast off pwise.

### Head

Beg at lower edge, using the thumb method and N, cast on 22 sts.
**Row 1 (WS):** Purl.
**Row 2:** K5, (m1, k1) 5 times, k3, (m1, k1) 5 times, k4 (32 sts).
**Rows 3 to 7:** Beg with a p row, work 5 rows in st-st.

**Row 8:** K4, (k2tog, k1) 3 times, k7, (k2tog, k1) 3 times, k3 (26 sts).
**Row 9:** Change to B and p 1 row.
**Row 10:** (K1 tbl) to end.
**Rows 11 to 17:** Beg with a p row, work 7 rows in st-st.
**Row 18:** (K4, k2tog, k1, k2tog, k4) twice (22 sts).
**Row 19 and foll 2 alt rows:** Purl.
**Row 20:** (K3, k2tog, k1, k2tog, k3) twice (18 sts).
**Row 22:** (K2, k2tog, k1, k2tog, k2) twice (14 sts).
**Row 24:** (K1, k2tog, k1, k2tog, k1) twice (10 sts).
Thread yarn through sts on needle, pull tight and secure by threading yarn a second time through sts.

### Large patch (make 2)

Using the thumb method and M, cast on 5 sts and work in g-st.
**Row 1 (RS):** Knit.
**Row 2:** K1, m1, k3, m1, k1 (7 sts).
**Rows 3 to 7:** Work 5 rows in g-st.
**Row 8:** (K1, m1) twice, k3, (m1, k1) twice (11 sts).
**Row 9:** Knit.
**Row 10:** K1, m1, k9, m1, k1 (13 sts).
**Rows 11 to 18:** Work 8 rows in g-st.
**Row 19:** K2tog, k to last 2 sts, k2tog (11 sts).
**Rows 20 and 21:** Rep row 19 twice more (7 sts).
Cast off in g-st.

## Legs
Fold cast-off stitches of legs in half and oversew. Sew up straight row ends and stuff legs. Sew legs to body.

## Head
Sew up row ends of head and stuff. With this seam at centre back, sew up lower edge.

## Patches
Using picture as a guide, sew a small patch to head and large patches to body at front and back using back stitch all the way round the outside edge of patches.

## Ears
Fold cast-off stitches of ears in half and oversew. Oversew row ends of each ear. Sew ears to head at each side.

## Features
Mark position of eyes with two pins on 4th row above muzzle with three clear knitted stitches in between. Embroider eyes in dark grey and work a vertical chain stitch for each eye, starting at marked position and finishing on second row above marked position. Work a second chain stitch on top of first chain stitch. Work two nostrils on muzzle, making a single chain stitch finishing on row above, with six clear knitted stitches in between (see page 171 for how to begin and fasten off the embroidery invisibly). Pin and sew head to Cow.

## Small patch (make 1)
Using the thumb method and M, cast on 4 sts and work in g-st.
**Row 1 (RS):** Knit.
**Row 2:** K1, m1, k to last st, m1, k1 (6 sts).
**Rows 3 and 4:** Rep rows 1 and 2 once (8 sts).
**Rows 5 to 16:** Work 12 rows in g-st.
**Row 17:** K2tog, k4, k2tog (6 sts).
**Row 18:** Knit.
**Row 19:** K2tog, k2, k2tog (4 sts).
Cast off in g-st.

## Ears (make 2)
Using the thumb method and M, cast on 14 sts and work in g-st, RS facing to beg.
**Rows 1 and 2:** Work 2 rows in g-st.
**Row 3:** K4, (k3tog) twice, k4 (10 sts).
Cast off in g-st.

## Making up Cow

### Tail
Make a twisted cord out of six strands of white yarn, each 24in (60cm) long (see page 171). Tie a knot 2in (5cm) from folded end and trim ends beyond knot to ½in (13mm).

### Body
Fold cast-on stitches of body in half and oversew. Fold cast-off stitches in half and oversew. Sew up shaped row ends and insert tail and attach securely. Stuff body and finish sewing up row ends.

# How to make Strange Little Man

## Boots, legs, body and head

### Right leg

Beg at sole of boot, using the thumb method and O, cast on 15 sts, WS facing to beg.

Place a marker on cast-on edge between the 5th and 6th st of the sts just cast on.

**Rows 1 to 3:** Beg with a p row, work 3 rows in st-st.

### Shape boot

**Row 4:** K3, (k2tog) 3 times, k6 (12 sts).

**Rows 5 to 13:** Beg with a p row, work 9 rows in st-st.

Break yarn and set aside.

### Left leg

Beg at sole of boot, using the thumb method and O, cast on 15 sts, WS facing to beg.

Place a marker on cast-on edge between the 10th and 11th st of the sts just cast on.

**Rows 1 to 3:** Beg with a p row, work 3 rows in st-st.

**Row 4:** K6, (k2tog) 3 times, k3 (12 sts).

**Rows 5 to 13:** Beg with a p row, work 9 rows in st-st.

### Join legs

**Row 14:** K across sts of left leg and then, with the same yarn, cont k across sts of right leg (24 sts).

Place a marker on first and last st of the last row.

**Rows 15 to 17:** Beg with a p row, work 3 rows in st-st.

**Rows 18 to 29:** Change to P for upper body and work 12 rows in st-st.

**Rows 30 to 39:** Change to D for head and work 10 rows in st-st.

### Shape top of head

**Row 40:** (K2tog, k1) to end (16 sts).

**Row 41:** Purl.

**Row 42:** (K2tog) to end (8 sts).

Thread yarn through sts on needle and leave loose.

## Skirt of tunic and belt

Beg at lower edge, using the thumb method and H, cast on 40 sts and beg in g-st, RS facing to beg.

**Rows 1 and 2:** Work 2 rows in g-st.

**Rows 3 to 6:** Beg with a k row, work 4 rows in st-st.

Change to M for belt and dec:

**Row 7:** K4, (k2tog, k4) to end (34 sts).

Cast off kwise.

## Arms (make 2)

Using the thumb method and H, cast on 12 sts, WS facing to beg.

**Rows 1 to 7:** Beg with a p row, work 7 rows in st-st.

**Rows 8 and 9:** Change to D and work 2 rows in st-st.

**Row 10:** (K2tog) to end (6 sts).

Thread yarn through sts on needle, pull tight and secure by threading yarn a second time through sts.

## Nose

Using the thumb method and D, cast on 5 sts.

**Row 1 (WS):** Purl.

Thread yarn through sts on needle, pull tight and secure by threading yarn a second time through sts.

## Hair

Beg at lower edge, using the thumb method and G, cast on 24 sts and work in g-st, RS facing to beg.

**Rows 1 to 12:** Work 12 rows in g-st.

**Shape crown**

**Row 13:** (K2tog, k1) to end (16 sts).

**Row 14:** Knit.

**Row 15:** (K2tog) to end (8 sts).

Thread yarn through sts on needle, pull tight and secure by threading yarn a second time through sts.

## Hat and feathers

**Hat**

Using the thumb method and O, cast on 22 sts, RS facing to beg.

**Rows 1 to 8:** Beg with a k row, work 8 rows in st-st and k the first and last st on every p row.

**Row 9:** (K2, k2tog) twice, k6, (k2tog, k2) twice (18 sts).

**Row 10:** Using the knitting-on method, cast on 12 sts at beg of row and p this row (30 sts).

**Rows 11 to 14:** Work 4 rows in st-st.

**Rows 15 and 16:** P 2 rows to mark fold line at top of hat.

**Shape crown**

**Row 17:** (K2tog, k3) to end (24 sts).

**Row 18 and foll alt row:** Purl.

**Row 19:** (K2tog, k2) to end (18 sts).

**Row 21:** (K2tog, k1) to end (12 sts).

**Row 22:** (P2tog) to end (6 sts).

Thread yarn through sts on needle, pull tight and secure by threading yarn a second time through sts.

**Peak of hat**

Using the thumb method and O, cast on 10 sts, WS facing to beg.

**Row 1 and foll alt row:** Purl.

**Row 2:** K2tog, k6, k2tog (8 sts).

**Row 4:** K1, m1, k6, m1, k1 (10 sts).

**Row 5:** Purl.

Cast off.

**Feathers**

**(Make one feather in L and one feather in Q)**

Using the thumb method and L or Q, cast on 12 sts, RS facing to beg.

Cast off pwise.

# Making up Strange Little Man

## Boots, legs, body and head

Make up boots, legs, body and head as for Jack.

## Skirt of tunic and belt

Sew up row ends of skirt of tunic and belt and place on doll. Sew belt to first row of upper body all the way round.

## Arms

Roll each arm up from row ends to row ends and sew in place. Gather round cast-on stitches, pull tight and secure. Sew arms to doll at each side.

## Features

Oversew row ends of cast-on edge of nose. Sew cast-on stitches of nose to 4th and 5th rows of head at centre front. Begin and fasten off features at top of head under hair and, using picture as a guide, mark position of eyes with two pins on row above nose with three clear knitted stitches in between. Embroider eyes in black, taking a vertical chain stitch for each eye, starting at marked position and finishing on row above. Embroider mouth in black using straight stitches. Shade cheeks with a red pencil.

## Hair

Make up hair as for Jack.

## Hat, peak and feathers

Sew up row ends of crown of hat and place hat on head. Sew hat to head across forehead and around back. With right side outside, fold peak and oversew cast-on and cast-off stitches. Sew peak to front of hat. Fold cast-off stitches of each feather in half and oversew. Using picture as a guide, sew feathers to hat.

## How to make Beans

### Bean (make 5)

Using the thumb method and a selection of colours from R, S and T, cast on 5 sts, WS facing to beg.

**Row 1 and foll alt row:** Purl.
**Row 2:** K1, m1, k3, m1, k1 (7 sts).
**Row 4:** K3, turn.
**Row 5:** S1p, p to end.
**Row 6:** Knit.
**Row 7:** P3, turn.
**Row 8:** S1k, k to end.
**Row 9:** Purl.
**Rows 10 to 15:** Rep rows 4 to 9 once.
**Row 16:** K2tog, k3, k2tog (5 sts).
**Row 17:** Purl.
Cast off.

## Making up Beans

With right side of knitting outside, bring cast-on and cast-off stitches together and sew up row ends and cast-on and cast-off stitches, leaving a gap. Stuff Beans, pushing stuffing in with tweezers or tip of scissors, and sew up gap.

## How to make Beanstalk

### Stalk

Using the thumb method, the circular needle and U, cast on 200 sts.

**Row 1 (WS):** P145 (55 sts rem), turn.

**Row 2:** S1k, k to end.

**Row 3:** P155 (45 sts rem), turn.

**Row 4:** S1k, k to end.

**Row 5:** P165 (35 sts rem), turn.

**Row 6:** S1k, k to end.

**Row 7:** P175 (25 sts rem), turn.

**Row 8:** S1k, k to end.

**Rows 9 to 23:** Work across all sts and beg with a p row, work 15 rows in st-st.

**Row 24:** *K12, (m1, k1) 4 times, k12, (k2tog) 4 times; rep from * 4 times more, k20 (200 sts).

**Row 25:** Purl.

Cast off loosely.

### Leaves (make 15)

Using the thumb method and U, cast on 1 st and beg in g-st.

**Row 1 (RS):** (K1, p1, k1) into front of first st (3 sts).

**Row 2:** Knit.

**Row 3:** Kfb, k1, kfb (5 sts).

**Rows 4 and 5:** Knit.

**Row 6:** Kfb, k to last st, kfb (7 sts).

**Rows 7 to 18:** Rep rows 4 to 6, 4 times more (15 sts).

**Rows 19 to 23:** Work 5 rows in g-st.

**Row 24:** (K2tog) twice, k7, (k2tog) twice (11 sts).

**Row 25 and foll alt row:** Knit.

**Row 26:** (K2tog) twice, k3, (k2tog) twice (7 sts).

**Row 28:** K2, k3tog, k2 (5 sts).

**Work stalk**

**Rows 29 to 46:** Beg with a k row, work 18 rows in st-st.

Thread yarn through sts on needle, pull tight and secure by threading yarn a second time through sts.

### Bean pods (make 12)

**Pod**

Using the thumb method and U, cast on 40 sts.

**Row 1 (WS):** Purl.

**Row 2:** (K2tog) twice, k32, (k2tog) twice (36 sts).

**Row 3:** P2tog, p32, p2tog (34 sts).

**Rows 4 and 5:** Work 2 rows in st-st.

Cast off.

**Stalk**

Using the thumb method and O, cast on 5 sts, WS facing to beg.

**Rows 1 to 15:** Beg with a p row, work 15 rows in st-st.

**Row 16:** (Kfb) to end (10 sts).

Cast off kwise.

## Making up Beanstalk

### Stalk

Roll up Beanstalk starting at base and roll from cast-on edge towards cast-off edge. Roll up short sections and pin in place, then sew cast-off stitches in place along length.

### Leaves and bean pods

Cut lengths of chenille stick the length of all the stalks for leaves and bean pods, and place each chenille stick length on wrong side of each stalk. Sew up row ends of stalk around chenille stick using mattress stitch and gather round stitches at top and bottom of chenille stick. Folding the bean pods in half, bring row ends together, oversew cast-on stitches and cast-off stitches and sew up row ends. Sew a bean pod to wide end of each bean pod stalk. Sew leaves and bean pods to Beanstalk.

# How to make Giant

## Feet, legs, body and head

### Right leg

Beg at sole of foot, using the thumb method and D, cast on 24 sts, WS facing to beg.

Place a marker on cast-on edge between the 8th and 9th st of the sts just cast on.

**Row 1 and foll alt row:** Purl.

**Row 2:** K4, (m1, k1) 4 times, (k1, m1) 4 times, k2, (m1, k1) 4 times, (k1, m1) 4 times, k2 (40 sts).

**Row 4:** K8, m1, (k2, m1) 4 times, k12, (m1, k2) twice, (k2, m1) twice, k4 (49 sts).

**Rows 5 to 17:** Beg with a p row, work 13 rows in st-st.

**Row 18:** K4, (k2tog, k1) 8 times, k21 (41 sts).

**Row 19:** Purl.

**Row 20:** (K1, k2tog) 8 times, k2, (k2tog, k1) twice, (k1, k2tog) twice, k3 (29 sts).

**Row 21:** P18, p2tog, p1, p2tog, p6 (27 sts).

**Rows 22 to 31:** Work 10 rows in st-st.

**Rows 32 and 33:** Change to V and work 2 rows in g-st.

**Rows 34 to 68:** Beg with a k row work 35 rows in st-st, ending with a RS row.

**Row 69:** P2tog, p to last 2 sts, p2tog (25 sts).

Break yarn and set aside.

### Left leg

Beg at sole of foot, using the thumb method and D, cast on 24 sts, WS facing to beg.

Place a marker on cast-on edge between the 16th and 17th st of the sts just cast on.

**Row 1 and foll alt row:** Purl.

**Row 2:** K2, (m1, k1) 4 times, (k1, m1) 4 times, k2, (m1, k1) 4 times, (k1, m1) 4 times, k4 (40 sts).

**Row 4:** K4, (m1, k2) twice, (k2, m1) twice, k12, (m1, k2) 4 times, m1, k8 (49 sts).

**Rows 5 to 17:** Beg with a p row, work 13 rows in st-st.

**Row 18:** K22, (k2tog, k1) 8 times, k3 (41 sts).

**Row 19:** Purl.

**Row 20:** K3, (k2tog, k1) twice, (k1, k2tog) twice, k2, (k2tog, k1) 8 times (29 sts).

**Row 21:** P6, p2tog, p1, p2tog, k18 (27 sts).

**Rows 22 to 31:** Work 10 rows in st-st.

**Rows 32 and 33:** Change to V and work 2 rows in g-st.

**Rows 34 to 68:** Beg with a k row, work 35 rows in st-st, ending with a RS row.

**Row 69:** P2tog, p to last 2 sts, p2tog (25 sts).

**Join legs**

**Row 70:** K across sts of left leg and then, with the same yarn, cont k across sts of right leg (50 sts).

**Rows 71 to 91:** Beg with a p row, work 21 rows in st-st.

**Rows 92 to 119:** Change to W for upper body and work 28 rows in st-st.

**Shape shoulders**

**Row 120:** K10, (k2tog) 3 times, k18, (k2tog) 3 times, k10 (44 sts).

**Row 121:** Change to D for head and p 1 row.

**Row 122:** K4, (m1, k4) to end (54 sts).

**Rows 123 to 145:** Beg with a p row, work 23 rows in st-st.

**Shape top of head**

**Row 146:** (K2tog, k4) to end (45 sts).

**Row 147 and foll 3 alt rows:** Purl.

**Row 148:** (K2tog, k3) to end (36 sts).

**Row 150:** (K2tog, k2) to end (27 sts).

**Row 152:** (K2tog, k1) to end (18 sts).

**Row 154:** (K2tog) to end (9 sts).

Thread yarn through sts on needle, pull tight and secure by threading yarn a second time through sts.

## Arms and hands (make 2)

Beg at shoulder, using the thumb method and W, cast on 6 sts.

**Row 1 (WS):** Purl.

**Row 2:** K1, m1, k to last st, m1, k1 (8 sts).

**Rows 3 to 12:** Rep first 2 rows 5 times more (18 sts).

**Row 13:** Purl.

**Rows 14 and 15:** Using the knitting-on method, cast on 2 sts at beg of next 2 rows (22 sts).

**Rows 16 to 39:** Work 24 rows in st-st.

**Rows 40 and 41:** Work 2 rows in g-st.

**Rows 42 to 47:** Change to D for hand and beg with a k row, work 6 rows in st-st.

**Shape thumb**

**Row 48:** K10, m1, k2, m1, k10 (24 sts).

**Row 49:** Purl.

**Row 50:** K11, m1, k2, m1, k11 (26 sts).

**Row 51:** P9, m1, p8, m1, p9 (28 sts).

**Row 52:** K18, turn.

**Row 53:** P8, turn and work on these 8 sts.

**Row 54:** Knit.

Break yarn and thread through sts, pull tight and secure by threading yarn a second time through sts.

With RS facing, rejoin yarn to sts half way across the row and k to end.

**Rows 55 to 58:** Push rem sts together and beg with a p row, work 4 rows in st-st, ending with a RS row (20 sts).

**Row 59:** (P2tog, p6, p2tog) twice (16 sts).

**Row 60:** (K2tog) to end (8 sts).

Thread yarn through sts on needle, pull tight and secure by threading yarn a second time through sts.

## Tunic

Beg at lower edge, using the thumb method and K, cast on 90 sts and beg in g-st, RS facing to beg.

**Rows 1 and 2:** Work 2 rows in g-st.

**Rows 3 to 20:** Beg with a k row work 18 rows in st-st and k the first 2 sts and last 2 sts on every p row.

**Row 21:** K5, (k2tog, k4) to last st, k1 (76 sts).

**Rows 22 to 37:** Beg with a p row, work 16 rows in st-st and k the first 2 sts and last 2 sts on every p row, ending with a RS row.

**Row 38:** K2, p17, k4, p30, k4, p17, k2.

**Row 39:** Knit.

**Row 40:** As row 38.

**Row 41:** K21, turn and work on these 21 sts.

**Row 42:** K2, p17, k2.

**Row 43:** K2, p2, k17.

**Row 44:** K2, p15, k4.

**Row 45:** K2, p3, k16.

**Row 46:** K2, p14, k5.

**Row 47:** K2, p4, k15.

**Row 48:** K2, p13, k6.

**Row 49:** K2, p5, k14.

**Row 50:** K2, p12, k7.

**Row 51:** K2, p6, k13.

**Row 52:** K2, p11, k8.

**Row 53:** K2, p7, k12.

**Row 54:** K2, p10, k9.

**Row 55:** K2, p8, k11.

**Row 56:** K2, p9, k10.

**Row 57:** K2, p9, k10.

**Row 58:** K2, p8, k11.

**Row 59:** K2, p10, k9.

**Row 60:** K2, p7, k12.

**Row 61:** K2, p11, k8.
**Row 62:** K2, p6, k13.
**Row 63:** K across all sts.
**Row 64:** K2, p6, k13.
Cast off kwise.
**Row 65:** With RS facing, rejoin yarn to rem sts and k34, turn and work on these 34 sts.
**Row 66:** K2, p30, k2.
**Row 67:** Knit.
**Rows 68 to 85:** Rep rows 66 and 67, 9 times more.
**Row 86:** K2, p6, k18, p6, k2.
**Row 87:** Knit.
Cast off 1 st kwise, cast off 6 sts pwise, cast off 18 sts kwise, cast off 6 sts pwise, cast off 2 sts kwise and fasten off.
**Row 88:** With RS facing rejoin yarn to rem sts and k to end (21 sts).
**Row 89:** K2, p17, k2.
**Row 90:** K17, p2, k2.
**Row 91:** K4, p15, k2.
**Row 92:** K16, p3, k2.
**Row 93:** K5, p14, k2.
**Row 94:** K15, p4, k2.
**Row 95:** K6, p13, k2.
**Row 96:** K14, p5, k2.
**Row 97:** K7, p12, k2.
**Row 98:** K13, p6, k2.
**Row 99:** K8, p11, k2.
**Row 100:** K12, p7, k2.
**Row 101:** K9, p10, k2.
**Row 102:** K11, p8, k2.
**Row 103:** K10, p9, k2.
**Row 104:** K10, p9, k2.
**Row 105:** K11, p8, k2.
**Row 106:** K9, p10, k2.
**Row 107:** K12, p7, k2.
**Row 108:** K8, p11, k2.
**Row 109:** K13, p6, k2.
**Row 110:** K across all sts.
**Row 111:** K13, p6, k2.
Cast off kwise.

## Sandals (make 2)
### Sole
Beg at outside edge, using the thumb method and G, cast on 56 sts and work in g-st, RS facing to beg.
**Rows 1 and 2:** Work 2 rows in g-st.
**Row 3:** (K2tog, k2) 3 times, k4, (k2, k2tog) 3 times, (k2tog, k2) 3 times, k4, (k2, k2tog) 3 times (44 sts).
**Rows 4 to 6:** Work 3 rows in g-st.
**Row 7:** (K2tog, k1) 3 times, k4, (k1, k2tog) 3 times, (k2tog, k1) 3 times, k4, (k1, k2tog) 3 times (32 sts).
**Rows 8 to 10:** Work 3 rows in g-st.
**Row 11:** (K2tog) 3 times, k4, (k2tog) 6 times, k4, (k2tog) 3 times (20 sts).
Cast off in g-st.
### Heel piece
Beg at lower edge, using the thumb method and G, cast on 30 sts and work in g-st, RS facing to beg.
**Rows 1 to 4:** Work 4 rows in g-st.
**Row 5:** K1, k2tog, k to last 3 sts, k2tog, k1 (28 sts).
**Row 6:** Knit.
**Rows 7 to 13:** Rep rows 5 and 6, 3 times more, then row 5 once (20 sts).
Cast off in g-st.
### Straps (make 2 pieces)
Using the thumb method and G, cast on 20 sts.
**Row 1 (RS):** Knit.
Cast off kwise.

## Beard
### Front of beard
Beg at top edge, using the thumb method and F, cast on 22 sts and work in rev st-st.
**Row 1 (RS):** Purl.
**Row 2:** K2, (m1, k2) to end (32 sts).
**Row 3:** Purl.
**Row 4:** K1, m1, k to last st, m1, k1 (34 sts).
**Rows 5 and 6:** Rep rows 3 and 4 once (36 sts).
**Row 7:** Purl.
**Row 8:** (K2tog) twice, k to last 4 sts, (k2tog) twice (32 sts).
**Row 9:** P2tog, p to last 2 sts, p2tog (30 sts).
**Rows 10 to 13:** Rep rows 8 and 9 twice more (18 sts).
**Row 14:** K2tog, k to last 2 sts, k2tog (16 sts).
**Row 15:** P2tog, p to last 2 sts, p2tog (14 sts).
**Rows 16 and 17:** Rep rows 14 and 15 once (10 sts).
**Row 18:** K1, (k2tog, k1) to end (7 sts).
Cast off in rev st-st.
### Back of beard
Beg at top edge, using the thumb method and F, cast on 22 sts and work in rev st-st.
**Row 1 (RS):** Purl.
**Row 2:** K2, (m1, k6) 3 times, m1, k2 (26 sts).
**Row 3:** Purl.
**Row 4:** K1, m1, k to last st, m1, k1 (28 sts).

**Rows 5 and 6:** Rep rows 3 and 4 once
(30 sts).
**Row 7:** Purl.
**Row 8:** K2tog, k to last 2 sts, k2tog
(28 sts).
**Row 9:** P2tog, p to last 2 sts, p2tog
(26 sts).
**Rows 10 to 17:** Rep rows 8 and 9, 4 times
(10 sts).
**Row 18:** K1, (k2tog, k1) to end (7 sts).
Cast off in rev st-st.

## Hair

Beg at outside edge using the thumb
method and F, cast on 40 sts and work
in g-st.
**Row 1 (RS):** Knit.
**Row 2:** K13, (m1, k1) 15 times, k12
(55 sts).
**Rows 3 and 4:** Work 2 rows in g-st.
**Row 5:** K46, turn.
**Row 6:** S1k, k36, turn.
**Row 7:** S1k, k to end.
**Row 8:** K 1 row.
**Rows 9 to 12:** Rep rows 5 to 8 once.
**Row 13:** (K2tog) 6 times, k31, (k2tog)
6 times (43 sts).
Cast off in g-st.

## Nose

Using the thumb method and D, cast on
6 sts.
**Row 1 (WS):** Purl.
**Row 2:** K1, (m1, k1) to end (11 sts).
**Rows 3 to 5:** Beg with a p row, work
3 rows in st-st.
**Row 6:** K4, k3tog, k4 (9 sts).
**Row 7:** P3, p3tog, p3 (7 sts).
**Row 8:** K2, k3tog, k2 (5 sts).
**Row 9:** P1, p3tog, p1 (3 sts).
Thread yarn through sts on needle,
pull tight and secure by threading yarn
a second time through sts.

# Making up Giant

### Feet, legs, body and head

Sew up row ends of each foot, and with
markers at tips of toes, oversew cast-on
stitches; leg seam will be ¾in (2cm) on
inside edge of heel. Stuff toes and feet,
then sew up row ends of legs and sew
round crotch. Stuff legs and sew up row
ends of body to half way up head. Stuff
body and head and pull stitches on thread
tight at top of head, fasten off and finish
sewing up row ends of head. To shape
neck, take a double length of yarn to
match upper body and sew a running
stitch around last row of upper body,
sewing in and out of every half stitch.
Pull yarn tight, knot ends and sew ends
into neck.

### Arms and hands

Sew up row ends of thumbs and then the
rest of hands and stuff thumbs and hands,
pushing stuffing into thumb with tweezers
or tip of scissors. Sew up row ends of arms
from hand to underarm and stuff arms.
With thumbs facing forwards, sew arms to
doll at either side, sewing the tops of arms
to row below neck.

### Tunic and belt

Sew up shoulder seams. Place tunic on
Giant and oversew centre front. Make a
twisted cord in rust using three strands
of yarn and beginning with the yarn
measuring 60in (150cm) long (see page
171). Tie cord around waist of Giant and
knot and trim ends.

### Sandals

Fold cast-on stitches of sole in half
and oversew row ends. Sew soles
to underneath feet. Sew all edges of
heel pieces to heels and outside edge
of sandals. Using picture as a guide,
sew on straps.

### Beard, hair, nose and eyes

Oversew outside edge of front and back
of beard and push a little stuffing into
beard. Pin and sew top edge of beard
to giant. Using picture as a guide, pin
and sew hair to Giant and sew sides
of beard to hair. Fold cast-on stitches
of nose in half and sew up. Place a tiny
ball of stuffing into nose and sew nose to
centre front of face. Mark position of eyes
with two pins on row at top of nose with
seven clear knitted stitches in between.
Embroider eyes in black, making a ring
of five small chain stitches around pins
and joining ring with a chain stitch (see
page 171 for how to begin and fasten
off the embroidery invisibly).

# How to make Hen, Golden Eggs and Nest

## Body and head

Beg at lower edge, using the thumb method and B, cast on 10 sts, WS facing to beg.

**Row 1 and foll 4 alt rows:** Purl.
**Row 2:** (K1, m1, k3, m1, k1) twice (14 sts).
**Row 4:** (K1, m1, k5, m1, k1) twice (18 sts).
**Row 6:** (K1, m1, k7, m1, k1) twice (22 sts).
**Row 8:** (K1, m1, k9, m1, k1) twice (26 sts).
**Row 10:** (K1, m1, k11, m1, k1) twice (30 sts).
**Row 11:** Purl.

### Shape tail

**Row 12:** K5, turn.
**Row 13:** S1p, p to end.
**Row 14:** K3, turn.
**Row 15:** S1p, p to end.
**Row 16:** Knit.
**Row 17:** P5, turn.
**Row 18:** S1k, k to end.
**Row 19:** P3, turn.
**Row 20:** S1k, k to end.
**Row 21:** Purl.
**Rows 22 and 23:** Cast off 8 sts at beg of next 2 rows (14 sts).
**Row 24:** K2tog, k to last 2 sts, k2tog (12 sts).
**Rows 25 to 27:** Beg with a p row, work 3 rows in st-st.

**Row 28:** (K2tog) to end (6 sts).
Thread yarn through sts on needle, pull tight and secure by threading yarn a second time through sts.

## Feet (make 2)

Using the thumb method and Q, cast on 4 sts, WS facing to beg.
**Rows 1 to 5:** Beg with a p row, work 5 rows in st-st.
Cast off kwise.

## Comb

Using the thumb method and L, cast on 6 sts.
Thread yarn through sts on needle, pull tight and secure by threading yarn a second time through sts.

## Beak

Using the thumb method and Q, cast on 6 sts.
**Row 1 (WS):** (P2tog) 3 times (3 sts).
Thread yarn through sts on needle, pull tight and secure by threading yarn a second time through sts.

## Crop

Using the thumb method and L, cast on 8 sts, RS facing to beg.
Cast off pwise.

## Eye pieces (make 2)

Using the thumb method and L, cast on 8 sts.
**Row 1 (WS):** P2, (p2tog) twice, p2 (6 sts).
**Row 2:** K1, (k2tog) twice, k1 (4 sts).
Thread yarn through sts on needle, pull tight and secure by threading yarn a second time through sts.

## Wings (make 2)

Using the thumb method and X, cast on 4 sts.
**Row 1 (WS):** (Pfb) to end (8 sts).
**Rows 2 to 5:** Beg with a k row, work 4 rows in st-st.
**Row 6:** K2tog, k4, k2tog (6 sts).
**Row 7:** Purl.
**Row 8:** K2tog, k2, k2tog (4 sts).
Thread yarn through sts on needle, pull tight and secure by threading yarn a second time through sts.

### Nest

Beg at centre of inside, using the thumb method and K, cast on 8 sts and work in g-st.

**Row 1 (RS):** (Kfb) to end (16 sts).
**Rows 2 and 3:** Work 2 rows in g-st.
**Row 4:** (Kfb, k1) to end (24 sts).
**Rows 5 and 6:** Work 2 rows in g-st.
**Row 7:** (Kfb, k2) to end (32 sts).
**Rows 8 to 22:** Work 15 rows in g-st.
**Row 23:** (K2tog, k2) to end (24 sts).
**Rows 24 and 25:** Work 2 rows in g-st.
**Row 26:** (K2tog, k1) to end (16 sts).
**Rows 27 and 28:** Work 2 rows in g-st.
**Row 29:** (K2tog) to end (8 sts).
Thread yarn through sts on needle, pull tight and secure by threading yarn a second time through sts.

### Eggs (make 3)

Using the thumb method and Q, cast on 7 sts.

**Row 1 (WS):** Purl.
**Row 2:** K1, (m1, k1) to end (13 sts).
**Rows 3 and 4:** P 1 row then k 1 row.
**Row 5:** P1, (p2tog, p1) to end (9 sts).
Thread yarn through sts on needle and leave loose.

## Making up Hen, Golden Eggs and Nest

### Body and head

Sew up row ends of body and head and cast-off stitches at back. Stuff body, pushing stuffing into head and tail. Fold cast-on stitches in half and oversew.

### Feet

Fold feet and oversew cast-on and cast-off stitches. Place Hen on a flat surface and position feet and sew in place.

### Comb, beak and crop

Sew comb to top of head all the way round lower edge. Sew beak to head all the way round. Fold crop in half and sew below beak.

### Eye pieces

Sew eye pieces to head around outside edge.

### Wings

Fold wings in half and oversew row ends. Sew to sides of Hen.

### Features

Embroider eyes using black on eyepieces with a tiny chain stitch (see page 171 for how to begin and fasten off the embroidery invisibly).

### Nest and eggs

Oversew row ends of Nest on right side and gather round cast-on stitches, pull tight and secure. Assemble inside of Nest and sew through two layers at centre to secure. Roll each Egg up from row ends to row ends, pull stitches on thread tight and secure. Gather round cast-on stitches, pull tight and secure and sew down row ends. Sew Eggs to centre of Nest.

## How to make Harp

### Frame

Using the thumb method and Q, cast on 6 sts, WS facing to beg.
Beg with a p row, work in st-st until piece measures 9½in (24cm).
Cast off.

### Base

Using the thumb method and Q, cast on 8 sts, WS facing to beg.
**Rows 1 to 13:** Beg with a p row, work 13 rows in st-st.
Cast off.

## Making up Harp

Cut two lengths of drinking straw, 3in (8cm) and 2in (5cm) long. Cut three chenille sticks 9in (23cm) long. Place three chenille sticks in a bundle and push them into cut lengths of drinking straw, one straw at each end with 4in (10cm) of chenille stick in the middle. Place knitted frame around straws and chenille sticks and sew up row ends by oversewing along length, enclosing straws and chenille sticks inside. Bend chenille sticks into a harp shape. Bring cast-on and cast-off stitches of base of Harp together and oversew. Sew up row ends at one side of base, stuff base and sew up row ends at the other side. Sew ends of frame of Harp to base and using picture as a guide, embroider strings in gold.

# How to make Axe

### Handle

Using the thumb method and F, cast on
6 sts, WS facing to beg.
Beg with a p row, work in st-st until
piece measures 3½in (9cm).
Cast off.

### Head of axe

Using the thumb method and X, cast
on 10 sts.
**Row 1 (WS):** Purl.
**Row 2:** K1, (k2tog) 4 times, k1 (6 sts).
**Rows 3 to 19:** Beg with a p row, work
17 rows in st-st.
**Row 20:** K1, (m1, k1) twice,
(k1, m1) twice, k1 (10 sts).
**Row 21:** Purl.
Cast off kwise.

## Making up Axe

Cut a 3in (8cm) length of drinking
straw. Place knitted handle around
straw and sew up row ends by
oversewing along length, enclosing
straw inside. Gather round top and
bottom, pull tight and secure. Place
head of Axe around handle with ¼in
(6mm) of handle showing at top.
Sew up row ends and sew head of
Axe to handle. Push a tiny ball of
stuffing into head of Axe, pushing
stuffing in with tweezers or tip of
scissors and oversew cast-on and
cast-off stitches.

There once lived a lovely princess called Snow White. She had a wicked stepmother who was very jealous of her because she wanted to be the most beautiful woman in the land, so she sent Snow White into the forest in the hope she'd never return…

# SNOW WHITE &
# THE SEVEN DWARFS

# Information you'll need

### Finished sizes
Snow White measures 8½in (22cm) high
Dwarfs measure 7in (18cm) high

### Materials
**Any DK (US: light worsted) yarn**
**Note:** amounts are approximate
5g navy blue (A)
15g pale pink (B)
15g white (C)
10g medium blue (D)
15g red (E)
10g yellow (F)
10g black (G)
15g royal blue (H)
10g brown (I)
10g fawn (J)
5g purple (K)
5g lilac (L)

5g orange (M)
5g pale blue (N)
5g petrol blue (O)
5g claret (P)
5g dark green (Q)
5g green (R)
5g bright pink (S)
5g mauve (T)
5g ginger (U)
5g silver grey (V)
5g dark grey (W)
5g gold (X)
Oddments of black, red, pale pink,
royal blue and gold for embroidery
1 pair of 3.25mm (UK10:US3) needles
and a spare needle of the same size
Knitters' blunt-ended pins and a needle
for sewing up

Tweezers for stuffing small parts (optional)
Acrylic toy stuffing
7 plastic drinking straws
4 chenille sticks
Red pencil for shading cheeks

### Tension
26 sts x 34 rows measure 4in (10cm)
square over st-st using 3.25mm needles
and DK yarn before stuffing.

### Working instructions
Sew up all row-end seams on right side
using mattress stitch, unless otherwise
stated; a one-stitch seam allowance has
been allowed for this.

# How to make Snow White

## Shoes, legs, body and head

Make shoes, legs, body and head as for Jack's Mother on page 44, using A for shoes, B for legs, C for lower body, D for upper body and B for neck and head.

## Skirt of dress

Beg at lower edge of skirt of dress, using the thumb method and E, cast on 72 sts and beg in g-st, RS facing to beg.

**Rows 1 to 4:** Work 4 rows in g-st.

**Rows 5 to 20:** Beg with a k row, work 16 rows in st-st.

**Row 21:** (K2tog, k4) to end (60 sts).

**Rows 22 to 26:** Beg with a p row, work 5 rows in st-st.

**Row 27:** (K2tog, k3) to end (48 sts).

**Rows 28 to 30:** Beg with a p row, work 3 rows in st-st.

**Row 31:** (K2tog, k2) to end (36 sts).

Cast off kwise.

## Sleeves, arms and hands (make 2)

Beg at shoulder, using the thumb method and F for sleeve, cast on 4 sts.

**Row 1 (WS):** Purl.

**Row 2:** K1 (m1, k1) to end (7 sts).

**Row 3:** Purl.

**Row 4:** K1, m1, k to last st, m1, k1 (9 sts).

**Rows 5 to 8:** Rep rows 3 and 4 twice more (13 sts).

Place a marker on first and last st of the last row.

**Row 9:** Purl.

**Rows 10 to 21:** Change to B for arm and beg with a k row, work 12 rows in st-st.

**Row 22:** K3, (k2tog, k3) twice (11 sts).

Place a marker on last row for the wrist gathering.

**Rows 23 to 27:** Beg with a p row, work 5 rows in st-st.

**Row 28:** K2tog, (k1, k2tog) to end (7 sts). Thread yarn through sts on needle, pull tight and secure by threading yarn a second time through sts.

## Sleeve frills (make 2)

Using the thumb method and F, cast on 20 sts, WS facing to beg.

**Rows 1 and 2:** P 1 row then k 1 row (this part is turned under).

**Picot row:** K2, (yf, k2tog) to end.

**Rows 4 to 6:** Beg with a k row, work 3 rows in st-st, ending with a k row.

Cast off kwise.

## Hair

Make hair as for Jack's Mother on page 45 using G.

## Neckband

Make neckband as for Jack's Mother on page 45 using D.

## Headscarf

Make headscarf as for Jack's Mother on page 45 using H.

# Making up Snow White

### Shoes, legs, body and head

Make up shoes, legs, body and head as for Jack's Mother on page 45.

### Skirt of dress

Make up skirt of dress as for Jack's Mother on page 45.

### Sleeves, arms and hands

Sew up row ends of hands and place a small ball of stuffing into hands, pushing stuffing in with tweezers or tip of scissors. Sew up sleeves from wrists to markers at underarm. Stuff sleeves and leave armholes open. To shape wrists, take a double length of pale pink and sew a gathering stitch around row with marker on at wrists, sewing in and out of every half stitch. Pull tight, knot yarn and sew ends into wrists.

### Sleeve frills

Turn hem under and sew in place. Place sleeve frills around arms and sew up row ends. Sew cast-off stitches of sleeve frills to first row of sleeve all the way round. Sew arms to doll at either side, sewing cast-on stitches at top of arms to second row below neck.

### Features, hair and embroidery

Work features and make up hair as for Jack's Mother on page 46. Using picture as a guide, embroider bodice in royal blue (see page 171 for how to begin and fasten off the embroidery invisibly).

### Neckband

Make up neckband as for Jack's Mother on page 46.

### Headscarf

Make up headscarf as for Jack's Mother on page 46.

# How to make Dwarfs

**Note:** make one dwarf in colours as shown and then six more dwarfs in a selection of colours for upper body, skirt of jacket, arms and hat, from K and L, F and M, N and O, E and P, Q and R, S and T. Work hair and beard for one dwarf in U, one in V and four more in C.

## Boots, legs, body and head

### Right leg
Beg at sole of boot, using the thumb method and I, cast on 10 sts.
Place a marker on cast-on edge between the 4th and 5th st of the sts just cast on.
**Row 1 (WS):** Purl.
**Row 2:** K1, (m1, k1) to end (19 sts).
**Rows 3 to 5:** Beg with a p row, work 3 rows in st-st.
**Shape boot**
**Row 6:** K1, (k2tog) 7 times, k4 (12 sts).
**Rows 7 to 9:** Beg with a p row, work 3 rows in st-st.
**Rows 10 to 19:** Change to J for leg and work 10 rows in st-st.
Break yarn and set aside.

### Left leg
Beg at sole of boot, using the thumb method and I, cast on 10 sts.
Place a marker on cast-on edge between the 6th and 7th st of the sts just cast on.
**Row 1 (WS):** Purl.
**Row 2:** K1, (m1, k1) to end (19 sts).
**Rows 3 to 5:** Beg with a p row, work 3 rows in st-st.
**Shape boot**
**Row 6:** K4, (k2tog) 7 times, k1 (12 sts).
**Rows 7 to 9:** Beg with a p row, work 3 rows in st-st.
**Rows 10 to 19:** Change to J for leg and work 10 rows in st-st.

## Join legs
**Row 18:** K across sts of left leg, and then with the same yarn cont k across sts of right leg (24 sts).
Place a marker on first and last st of the last row.
**Rows 19 to 21:** Beg with a p row, work 3 rows in st-st.
**Rows 22 to 33:** Change to D for upper body and beg with a k row, work 12 rows in st-st.
**Rows 34 to 43:** Change to B for head and work 10 rows in st-st.

## Shape top of head
**Row 44:** (K2tog, k1) to end (16 sts).
**Row 45:** Purl.
**Row 46:** (K2tog) to end (8 sts).
Thread yarn through sts on needle, and leave loose.

## Boot tops (make 2)
Using the thumb method and I, cast on 18 sts, RS facing to beg.
Cast off pwise.

## Skirt of tunic and belt

Beg at lower edge, using the thumb method and H, cast on 36 sts and beg in g-st, RS facing to beg.

**Rows 1 and 2:** Work 2 rows in g-st.
**Rows 3 to 6:** Beg with a k row, work 4 rows in st-st.
Change to G for belt and dec:
**Row 7:** K2, k2tog, (k4, k2tog) to last 2 sts, k2 (30 sts).
Cast off kwise.

## Arms and hands

Using the thumb method and colour to match skirt of tunic, cast on 5 sts.
**Row 1 (WS):** Purl.
**Row 2:** K1, (m1, k1) to end (9 sts).
**Rows 3 to 11:** Beg with a p row, work 9 rows in st-st.
**Rows 12 and 13:** Change to B and work 2 rows in st-st.
**Row 14:** (K2tog, k1) to end (6 sts).
Thread yarn through sts on needle, pull tight and secure by threading yarn a second time through sts.

### Hair

Beg at lower edge, using the thumb method and C, cast on 24 sts and work in g-st, RS facing to beg.
**Rows 1 to 12:** Work 12 rows in g-st.
**Shape crown**
**Row 13:** (K2tog, k1) to end (16 sts).
**Row 14:** Knit.
**Row 15:** (K2tog) to end (8 sts).
Thread yarn through sts on needle, pull tight and secure by threading yarn a second time through sts.

### Hat

Using the thumb method and colour to match upper body, cast on 32 sts, RS facing to beg.
**Rows 1 to 8:** Beg with a k row, work 8 rows in st-st.
**Row 9:** (K2tog, k2) to end (24 sts).

**Rows 10 to 12:** Beg with a p row, work 3 rows in st-st.
**Row 13:** (K2tog, k2) to end (18 sts).
**Rows 14 to 16:** Beg with a p row, work 3 rows in st-st.
**Row 17:** (K2tog, k1) to end (12 sts).
**Row 18:** Purl.
**Row 19:** (K2tog) to end (6 sts).
Thread yarn through sts on needle, pull tight and secure by threading yarn a second time through sts.

### Beard

Beg at lower edge, using the thumb method and C, cast on 4 sts and work in g-st, RS facing to beg.
**Rows 1 to 6:** Work 6 rows in g-st.
**Row 7:** K3, m1, k1 (5 sts).
**Rows 8 to 10:** Work 3 rows in g-st.
**Row 11:** K4, m1, k1 (6 sts).
**Rows 12 to 22:** Work 11 rows in g-st.

**Row 23:** K3, k2tog, k1 (5 sts).
**Rows 24 to 26:** Work 3 rows in g-st.
**Row 27:** K2, k2tog, k1 (4 sts).
**Rows 28 to 33:** Work 6 rows in g-st, ending with a RS row.
Cast off in g-st.

### Pick, spade and lantern

**Note:** Make a selection of picks, spades and lanterns, one for each dwarf.
**Head of pick**
Using V, cast on 3 sts, WS facing to beg.
**Rows 1 and 3:** Purl.
**Row 2:** K1, m1, k1, m1, k1 (5 sts).
**Row 4:** K1, m1, k3, m1, k1 (7 sts).
**Rows 5 to 13:** Beg with a p row, work 9 rows in st-st.
**Row 14:** K1, k2tog, k1, k2tog, k1 (5 sts).
**Row 15:** Purl.
**Row 16:** K1, k3tog, k1 (3 sts).
**Row 17:** Purl.

Thread yarn through sts on needle, pull tight and secure by threading yarn a second time through sts.

### Handle of pick

Using V, cast on 6 sts, WS facing to beg.

**Rows 1 to 7:** Beg with a p row, work 7 rows in st-st.

Change to W and work in st-st until work measures 3¼in (8cm) from beg.

Cast off in st-st.

### Head of spade

Using W, cast on 16 sts, WS facing to beg.

**Rows 1 to 5:** Beg with a p row, work 5 rows in st-st.

**Row 6:** K2, (k2tog) twice, k4, (k2tog) twice, k2 (12 sts).

**Rows 7 to 9:** Beg with a p row, work 3 rows in st-st.

**Row 10:** K1, (k2tog) twice, k2, (k2tog) twice, k1 (8 sts).

**Row 11:** (P2tog) to end (4 sts).

### Handle of spade

Using W, cast on 6 sts, WS facing to beg.

**Rows 1 to 5:** Beg with a p row, work 5 rows in st-st.

Change to V and work in st-st until work measures 2in (5cm) from beg.

Cast off in st-st.

### Top of handle

Using V, cast on 6 sts, WS facing to beg.

Beg with a p row, work st-st until work measures 1½in (4cm).

Cast off in st-st.

### Lantern

Using the thumb method and G, cast on 6 sts.

**Row 1 (WS):** Purl.

**Row 2:** (Kfb) to end (12 sts).

**Row 3:** Knit.

**Rows 4 and 5:** Join on X and beg with a k row, work 2 rows in st-st.

**Rows 6 and 7:** Carry yarn loosely up side of work and using G, work 2 rows in g-st.

**Rows 8 to 11:** Rep rows 4 to 7 once.

**Rows 12 and 13:** Cont in G and k 1 row, then p 1 row.

**Row 14:** (K2tog, k1) to end (8 sts).

**Rows 15 and 16:** P 1 row, then k 1 row.

**Row 17:** (P2tog) to end (4 sts).

Thread yarn through sts on needle, pull tight and secure by threading yarn a second time through sts.

### Pole of lantern

Using W, cast on 6 sts, WS facing to beg.

Beg with a p row, work in st-st until work measures 6in (15cm).

Cast off in st-st.

# Making up Dwarfs

### Boots, legs, body and head

Sew up row ends of boots and, with markers at tips of toes, oversew cast-on stitches; leg seam will be ¼in (6mm) on inside edge of heel. Place a ball of stuffing into toe of each boot, pushing stuffing in with tweezers or tip of scissors. Sew up row ends of legs and sew round crotch. Stuff legs, pushing stuffing in with tweezers or tip of scissors. Sew up row ends of body, up to halfway up head. Stuff body and head and pull stitches on thread tight, fasten off and finish sewing up row ends. To shape neck, take a double length of yarn to match upper body and sew a running stitch round last row of upper body, sewing in and out of every half stitch. Pull tight, knot yarn and sew ends into neck.

### Skirt of tunic and belt

Sew up row ends of skirt of tunic and belt and place on doll. Sew belt to first row of upper body all the way round.

### Arms

Sew up row ends of arms leaving a gap and stuff, pushing stuffing in with tweezers or tip of scissors. Sew up gap and gather round cast-on stitches, pull tight and secure. Sew arms to doll at each side.

### Features

Mark position of eyes with two pins on 5th row above neck with two clear knitted stitches in between. Begin and fasten off features at top of head under hair and embroider eyes in black, working a vertical chain stitch for each eye, starting at marked position and finishing on the row above. Embroider nose in pale pink on row below eyes, making a bundle of five horizontal stitches over one stitch. Shade cheeks with a red pencil. Embroider buckle in gold using straight stitches (see page 171 for how to start and fasten off invisibly for the embroidery).

### Hair

Make up hair as for Jack on page 43.

### Hat

Sew up row ends of hat, lightly stuff top of hat and place hat on head. Pin and sew lower edge of hat to head.

### Beard

Sew a gathering stitch along straight row ends and gather top edge of beard. Sew beard around face and sew ends of beard to hair at both sides.

## Pick

Cut a length of drinking straw ½in (13mm) long and two lengths of chenille stick each 1½in (4cm) long. Place chenille sticks inside straw and slide straw to middle. Place head of pick around straw and chenille sticks and oversew row ends along length, enclosing straw and chenille sticks inside. Bend tips of head of pick up. To make handle, cut a length of drinking straw 3in (7.5cm) long, place handle of pick around straw and oversew row ends along the length, enclosing straw inside. Gather round cast-off stitches at top of handle, pull tight and secure. Sew head of pick to handle at centre of lower edge. Sew pick to Dwarf.

## Spade

Sew up row ends of spade with seam at centre back and set aside. Cut a length of drinking straw 2in (5cm) long and two lengths of chenille stick each 3½in (9cm) long. Place chenille sticks inside straw and slide straw to top end. Bend chenille sticks out and round in the shape of a spade and place inside head of spade. Oversew cast-on stitches at top of head of spade. To make handle, place long piece of knitting around straw and oversew along length, enclosing straw inside. Sew head of spade to handle at lower edge. Cut a length of drinking straw 1in (2.5cm) long, place short piece of knitting around straw and oversew along length, enclosing straw inside. Gather round both ends of short piece, pull tight and secure. Sew short piece across top of handle. Sew spade to Dwarf.

## Lantern

Gather round cast-on stitches of lantern and sew up row ends, leaving a gap. Stuff, pushing stuffing in with tweezers or tip of scissors, and sew up gap. Embroider vertical lines around lantern. To make pole, cut a length of drinking straw 5½in (14cm) long, place pole of lantern around straw and oversew row ends along the length, enclosing straw inside. Gather round top and bottom, pull tight and secure. Sew lantern to pole ½in (13mm) below top of pole. Sew pole to Dwarf.

Cinderella lived with her stepmother and two ugly stepsisters. They treated Cinderella terribly, dressing her in rags and making her do all the cleaning. One day, the family were invited to a ball at the King's palace, but the wicked stepmother wouldn't let Cinderella go...

# CINDERELLA

# Information you'll need

## Finished sizes

Cinderella measures 8½in (22cm) high
Fairy Godmother measures 9in (23cm) high
Prince measures 8½in (22cm) high
Courtier with glass slipper measures 6¾in (17cm) high

## Materials

**Any DK (US: light worsted) yarn**
**Note:** amounts are approximate
10g dark grey (A)
20g pale pink (B)
10g white (C)
10g duck egg blue (D)
10g silver grey (E)
10g fawn (F)
20g red (G)
15g gold (H)
5g Air Force blue (I)
5g purple (J)
10g cerise (K)
30g medium blue (L)
5g lemon (M)
5g black (N)
20g petrol blue (O)
5g brown (P)
5g dark purple (Q)
5g ginger (R)
5g ice blue (S)

Oddments of black, red, pale pink and gold for embroidery
1 pair of 3.25mm (UK10:US3) needles and 1 spare needle of the same size
Knitters' blunt-ended pins and a needle for sewing up
Tweezers for stuffing small parts (optional)
Acrylic toy stuffing
Red pencil for shading cheeks
1 drinking straw
Small amount of white felt
Fabric glue
Sewing needle and white thread

## Tension

26 sts x 34 rows measure 4in (10cm) square over st-st using 3.25mm needles and DK yarn before stuffing.

## Working instructions

Sew up all row-end seams on right side using mattress stitch, unless otherwise stated; a one-stitch seam allowance has been allowed for this.

# How to make Cinderella in Rags

## Shoes, legs, body and head

### Right shoe and leg

Beg at sole of shoe, using the thumb method and A, cast on 14 sts.

Place a marker on cast-on edge between the 5th and 6th st of the sts just cast on.

**Row 1 (WS):** Purl.

**Row 2:** K2, (m1, k2) to end (20 sts).

**Rows 3 to 7:** Beg with a p row, work 5 rows in st-st.

### Shape shoe

**Row 8:** (K1, k2tog) twice, k2, (k2tog, k1) twice, k6 (16 sts).

**Row 9:** Purl.

Change to B for leg and dec:

**Row 10:** (K2, k2tog) twice, k8 (14 sts).

**Rows 11 to 33:** Beg with a p row, work 23 rows in st-st.

Break yarn and set aside.

### Left shoe and leg

Beg at sole of shoe, using the thumb method and A, cast on 14 sts.

Place a marker on cast-on edge between the 9th and 10th st of the sts just cast on.

**Row 1 (WS):** Purl.

**Row 2:** K2, (m1, k2) to end (20 sts).

**Rows 3 to 7:** Beg with a p row, work 5 rows in st-st.

### Shape shoe

**Row 8:** K7, (k2tog, k1) twice, (k1, k2tog) twice, k1 (16 sts).

**Row 9:** Purl.

Change to B for leg and dec:

**Row 10:** K8, (k2tog, k2) twice (14 sts).

**Rows 11 to 33:** Beg with a p row, work 23 rows in st-st.

### Join legs

**Row 34:** Change to C for lower body and k across sts of left leg, and then with the same yarn cont k across sts of right leg (28 sts).

**Rows 35 to 41:** Beg with a p row, work 7 rows in st-st.

**Rows 42 to 55:** Change to D for upper body and work 14 rows in st-st.

**Rows 56 and 57:** Change to B for head and work 2 rows in st-st.

**Row 58:** *K4, (m1, k2) 4 times, k2; rep from * once (36 sts).

**Rows 59 to 73:** Beg with a p row, work 15 rows in st-st.

### Shape top of head

**Row 74:** (K2tog, k2) to end (27 sts).

**Row 75 and foll alt row:** Purl.

**Row 76:** (K2tog, k1) to end (18 sts).

**Row 78:** (K2tog) to end (9 sts).

Thread yarn through sts on needle and leave loose.

## Sleeves, hands and cuffs (make 2)

Make sleeves, hands and cuffs as for Jack's Mother on page 45, using D for sleeves, B for hands and D for cuffs.

## Skirt of dress and apron bib

Beg at lower edge of skirt of dress, using the thumb method and E, cast on 60 sts and beg in g-st, RS facing to beg.

**Rows 1 and 2:** Work 2 rows in g-st.

**Rows 3 to 18:** Join in D and beg with a k row, work 16 rows in st-st in stripe, 2 rows D, then 2 rows E, and do this alternately, carrying yarn loosely up side of work. Cont in stripe as set and dec:

**Row 19:** (K2tog, k3) to end (48 sts).

**Rows 20 to 24:** Beg with a p row, work 5 rows in st-st in stripe.

Change to C for waistband of apron and dec:

**Row 25:** (K2tog, k2) to end (36 sts).

**Rows 26 and 27:** Work 2 rows in g-st, ending with a RS row.

### Shape back

**Row 28:** Cast off 12 sts kwise, k11 (12 sts now on RH needle), cast off 12 sts and fasten off (12 sts).

### Work bib

**Row 29:** Rejoin C to rem sts and k 1 row.

**Row 30:** K2, p to last 2 sts, k2.

**Row 31:** Knit.

**Rows 32 to 37:** Rep rows 30 and 31, 3 times more, ending with a RS row.

Cast off kwise.

## Hair

Make hair as for Jack's Mother on page 45 using F.

## Apron

Beg at lower edge, using the thumb method and C, cast on 14 sts and beg in g-st, RS facing to beg.
**Rows 1 and 2:** Work 2 rows in g-st.
**Row 3:** Knit.
**Row 4:** K2, p10, k2.
**Rows 5 to 18:** Rep rows 3 and 4, 7 times more.
Cast off kwise.

## Neck strap

Using the thumb method and C, cast on 34 sts.
**Row 1 (RS):** Knit.
Cast off kwise.

## Bow

Using the thumb method and C, cast on 35 sts, RS facing to beg.
Cast off pwise.

## Patches

Make one patch in G and one patch in H. Using the thumb method and G or H, cast on 4 sts and work in g-st, RS facing to beg.
**Rows 1 to 3:** Work 3 rows in g-st.
Cast off in g-st.

## Headscarf

Make headscarf as for Jack's Mother on page 45 using I.

# Making up Cinderella in Rags

### Shoes, legs, body and head

Sew up row ends of shoes and, with markers at tips of toes, oversew cast-on stitches; leg seam will be ⅓in (8mm) on inside edge of heel. Sew up ankles and place a ball of stuffing into toes. Sew up row ends of legs and sew round crotch. Stuff legs and sew up body seam. Stuff body and sew up row ends of head to halfway up head. Stuff head and pull stitches on a thread tight at top of head, fasten off and finish sewing up row ends. To shape neck, take a double length of yarn in colour to match upper body and sew a running stitch round last row of upper body, sewing in and out of every half stitch. Pull tight, knot yarn and sew ends into neck.

### Sleeves, hands and cuffs

Make up sleeves, hands and cuffs as for Jack's Mother on page 45.

### Skirt of dress and apron bib

Sew up row ends of skirt of dress and place on doll. Sew cast-off stitches of waist to first row of upper body.

### Features and hair

Work features and make up hair as for Jack's Mother on page 46.

### Apron, neck strap and bow

Place apron at centre front of skirt and sew cast-off stitches to waistband. Then sew lower edge of apron to skirt. Sew one end of neck strap to bib, take around neck and sew other end to other side of bib. Shape bow into a bow shape, sew together and sew to back of waistband.

### Patches

Using picture as a guide, sew patches to apron using black.

### Headscarf

Make up headscarf as for Jack's Mother on page 46.

# How to make Fairy Godmother

## Shoes, legs, body and head

Make shoes, legs, body and head as for Cinderella in Rags, using J for shoes, B for legs, C for lower body, K for upper body and B for head.

## Skirt

Beg at lower edge, using the thumb method and C, cast on 70 sts, WS facing to beg.

**Rows 1 and 2:** P 1 row then k 1 row (this part is turned under).

**Picot edge:** K2, (yf, k2tog) to end.

**Rows 4 and 5:** K 1 row then p 1 row.

**Rows 6 and 7:** Change to L and work 2 rows in g-st.

**Row 8:** K4, (k2tog, k4) to end (59 sts).

**Row 9:** K1, (p1, k1) to end (this row will be referred to as moss-st and is repeated).

**Rows 10 to 27:** Work 18 rows in moss-st.

**Rows 28 to 37:** Change to K and work 10 rows in moss-st.

**Row 38:** K1, p1, k1, (p3tog, moss-st 7) 5 times, p3tog, k1, p1, k1 (47 sts).

**Rows 39 to 41:** Work 3 rows in moss-st.

**Row 42:** K1, (p3tog, k1, p1, k1) 7 times, p3tog, k1 (31 sts).

Cast off in moss-st.

## Sleeves and hands (make 2)

Make sleeves and hands as for Jack's Mother on page 45, using K for sleeves and B for hands.

## Hair

Make hair as for Jack's Mother on page 45, using C.

## Bun

Using the thumb method and C, cast on 12 sts and work in g-st, RS facing to beg.

**Rows 1 and 2:** Work 2 rows in g-st.

**Row 3:** (Kfb, k1) to end (18 sts).

**Rows 4 to 8:** Work 5 rows in g-st.

**Row 9:** (K2tog, k1) to end (12 sts).

**Row 10:** (K2tog) to end (6 sts).

Thread yarn through sts on needle, pull tight and secure by threading yarn a second time through sts.

## Collar

Beg at lower edge, using the thumb method and J, cast on 63 sts, WS facing to beg.

**Rows 1 and 2:** P 1 row then k 1 row (this part is turned under).

**Picot edge:** K1, (yf, k2tog) to end.

**Rows 4 and 5:** K 1 row then p 1 row.

**Rows 6 and 7:** Work 2 rows in g-st.

**Row 8:** K3, (k2tog, k3) to end (51 sts).

**Row 9:** K1, (p1, k1) to end (this row will be referred to as moss-st and is repeated).

**Rows 10 to 14:** Work 5 rows in moss-st.

**Row 15:** K2, (k3tog, k1) to last st, k1 (27 sts).

**Row 16:** Work 1 row in moss-st.

Cast off in moss-st.

## Wings (make 2)

Beg at centre back using the thumb method and L, cast on 8 sts.

**Row 1 (WS):** Purl.

**Row 2:** (K1, m1) twice, k to last 2 sts, (m1, k1) twice (12 sts).

**Rows 3 to 16:** Rep rows 1 and 2, 7 times more (40 sts).

**Rows 17 to 35:** Beg with a p row, work 19 rows in st-st.

**Row 36:** (K2tog, k16, k2tog) twice (36 sts).

**Row 37 and foll 2 alt rows:** Purl.

**Row 38:** *(K2tog) twice, k10, (k2tog) twice; rep from * once (28 sts).
**Row 40:** *(K2tog) twice, k6, (k2tog) twice; rep from * once (20 sts).
**Row 42:** *(K2tog) twice, k2, (k2tog) twice; rep from * once (12 sts).
**Row 43:** (P2tog) to end (6 sts).
Thread yarn through sts on needle, pull tight and secure by threading yarn a second time through sts.

## Wand
Using the thumb method and C, cast on 5 sts, WS facing to beg.
Beg with a p row, work in st-st for 3in (8cm).
Cast off.

*cinderella*

# Making up
# Fairy Godmother

### Shoes, legs, body and head
Make up shoes, legs, body and head as for Cinderella in Rags.

### Skirt
Turn under cast-on stitches along picot row and sew in place. Sew up row ends of skirt and place on doll. Sew cast-off stitches of skirt to first row of upper body all the way round.

### Sleeves and hands
Make up sleeves and hands as for Jack's Mother on page 45.

### Features
Work features as for Jack's Mother on page 46.

### Hair and bun
Make up hair as for Jack's Mother on page 46. Sew up row ends of bun and stuff, pushing stuffing in with tweezers or tip of scissors. Sew lower edge of bun to top of head all the way round.

### Collar
Turn under cast-on stitches along picot row and sew in place. Place collar around neck and, with seam at centre back, sew up row ends. Sew cast-off stitches of collar to neck.

### Wings
Fold wings, bringing straight row ends together, and sew up. Stuff wings lightly and oversew shaped row ends. Place wings side by side and sew up centre to join wings together. Sew wings to back of Fairy Godmother.

### Wand
Cut a 2¾in (7cm) length of drinking straw. Place knitted wand around straw and sew up row ends by oversewing along length, enclosing straw inside. Gather round top and bottom, pull tight and secure. Trace diagram below and cut two star shapes from white felt. Cover one side of each of the cut star shapes with fabric glue, place stick of wand between them and stick them together matching all edges. Oversew around outer edge of star shape with sewing needle and thread. Leave to dry, then sew wand to right hand.

# How to make Cinderella in Ball Gown

### Shoes, legs, body and head
Make shoes, legs, body and head as for Jack's Mother on page 44, using C for shoes, B for legs, C for lower body, H for upper body and B for neck and head.

### Skirt
Beg at lower edge, using the thumb method and M, cast on 60 sts and beg in g-st, RS facing to beg.

**Rows 1 to 8:** Work 8 rows in g-st.
**Rows 9 to 28:** Join on C and beg with a k row, work 20 rows in st-st in stripe, 2 rows C, then 2 rows M, and do this alternately, carrying yarn loosely up side of work. Cont in stripe as set and shape.
**Row 29:** (K2tog, k3) to end (48 sts).
**Rows 30 to 34:** Beg with a p row, work 5 rows in st-st in stripe.
**Row 35:** (K2tog, k2) to end (36 sts).
**Row 36:** Purl.
Cast off in M.

### Train of dress
Beg at lower edge, using H, cast on 46 sts and beg in g-st, RS facing to beg.
**Rows 1 to 6:** Work 6 rows in g-st.
**Rows 7 to 36:** Beg with a k row, work 30 rows in st-st and k the first 2 sts and last 2 sts on every p row.
**Row 37:** K2, (k2tog, k2) to end (35 sts). Cast off pwise.

### Sleeves, hands and cuffs (make 2)
Make sleeves, hands and cuffs as for Jack's Mother on page 45, using H for sleeves and cuffs and B for hands.

### Hair
Make hair as for Jack's Mother on page 45 using F.

### Neckband
Make neckband as for Jack's Mother on page 45, using H.

### Bun (make 2)
Using the thumb method and F, cast on 12 sts and work in g-st, RS facing to beg.
**Rows 1 and 2:** Work 2 rows in g-st.
**Row 3:** (Kfb, k2) to end (16 sts).
**Rows 4 to 6:** Work 3 rows in g-st.
**Row 7:** (K2tog, k2) to end (12 sts).
**Row 8:** (K2tog) to end (6 sts).
Thread yarn through sts on needle, pull tight and secure by threading yarn a second time through sts.

# Making up Cinderella in Ball Gown

### Shoes, legs, body and head

Make up shoes, legs, body and head as for Jack's Mother on page 45.

### Skirt of dress and train

Sew up row ends of skirt of dress and place on doll. Sew cast-off stitches of skirt to first row of upper body. Place train around waist and join at centre front. Sew cast-off stitches of train to row above skirt all the way round.

### Sleeves, hands and cuffs

Make up sleeves, hands and cuffs as for Jack's Mother on page 45.

### Neckband

Make up neckband as for Jack's Mother on page 46.

### Features

Work features as for Jack's Mother on page 46.

### Hair and buns

Make up hair as for Jack's Mother on page 46. Sew up row ends of each bun, stuff and sew buns to sides of hair.

# How to make Prince

### Shoes, legs, body and head

Make shoes, legs, body and head as for Cinderella in Rags, using N for shoes, C for legs, A for lower body, O for upper body and B for head.

### Breeches

#### First leg

Beg at lower edge, using the thumb method and O, cast on 20 sts, RS facing to beg.

**Rows 1 and 2:** P 1 row then k 1 row.

**Row 3:** K9, m1, k2, m1, k9 (22 sts).

**Rows 4 to 14:** Beg with a p row, work 11 rows in st-st.

**Rows 15 and 16:** Cast off 2 sts at beg of next 2 rows (18 sts).

Break yarn and set aside.

#### Second leg

Work as first leg but do not break yarn.

#### Join legs

**Row 17:** With RS facing, k across sts of second leg, and then with the same yarn cont k across sts of first leg (36 sts).

**Rows 18 to 24:** Beg with a p row, work 7 rows in st-st.

Cast off.

### Tunic

Beg at lower edge, using the thumb method and G, cast on 52 sts and beg in g-st, RS facing to beg.

**Rows 1 to 4:** Work 4 rows in g-st.

**Rows 5 to 8:** Change to O and beg with a k row, work 4 rows in st-st.

**Row 9:** (K10, k2tog, k2, k2tog, k10) twice (48 sts).

**Rows 10 to 12:** Work 3 rows in st-st.

**Row 13:** (K9, k2tog, k2, k2tog, k9) twice (44 sts).

**Rows 14 to 16:** Work 3 rows in st-st.

**Row 17:** (K8, k2tog, k2, k2tog, k8) twice (40 sts).

**Rows 18 to 26:** Beg with a p row, work 9 rows in st-st.

**Row 27:** K1, k2tog, (k2, k2tog) to last st, k1 (30 sts).

Cast off pwise.

### Sleeves and hands

Make sleeves and hands as for Jack's Mother on page 45, using O for sleeves and B for hands.

### Cuffs

Using the thumb method and G, cast on 18 sts and work in g-st, RS facing to beg.

**Rows 1 and 2:** Work 2 rows in g-st.

**Row 3:** K3, (k2tog, k3) to end (15 sts).

Cast off in g-st.

### Hair

Make hair as for Jack's Mother on page 45, using P.

## Crown

Using the thumb method and M, cast on 25 sts, WS facing to beg.
**Rows 1 and 2:** P 1 row then k 1 row.
**Picot row:** K1, (yf, k2tog) to end.
**Rows 4 and 5:** K1 row then p 1 row.
Cast off.

## Collar of cloak

Using the thumb method and G, cast on 24 sts and work in g-st.
**Row 1 (RS):** Knit.
**Row 2:** *K2, (m1, k1) 9 times, k1; rep from * once (42 sts).
**Row 3:** K38, turn.
**Row 4:** S1k, k33, turn.
**Row 5:** S1k, k29, turn.
**Row 6:** S1k, k25, turn.
**Row 7:** S1k, k to end.
**Row 8:** K3, (m1, k3) to end (55 sts).
Cast off in g-st.

## Cloak

Using the thumb method and G, cast on 30 sts and work in g-st, RS facing to beg.
**Rows 1 to 18:** Work 18 rows in g-st.
**Row 19:** K2, k2tog, k to last 4 sts, k2tog, k2 (28 sts).
**Rows 20 to 24:** Work 5 rows in g-st.
**Rows 25 to 54:** Rep rows 19 to 24, 5 times more (18 sts).
Cast off in g-st.

## Brooch

Using the thumb method and H, cast on 9 sts.
**Row 1 (WS):** Purl.
Thread yarn through sts on needle, pull tight and secure by threading yarn a second time through sts, then oversew row ends.

## Making up Prince

### Shoes, legs, body and head

Make up shoes, legs, body and head as for Cinderella in Rags.

### Breeches

Sew up row ends of each leg from lower edge to crotch. Sew round crotch by oversewing and sew up row ends at centre back. Place breeches on doll and sew cast-off stitches to first row of upper body all the way round.

### Tunic

Place tunic around doll and with seam at centre back, sew up row ends. Sew cast-off stitches of tunic to neck.

### Sleeves, hands and cuffs

Sew up row ends of hands and place a small ball of stuffing into hands, pushing stuffing in with tweezers or tip of scissors. Sew up sleeves from wrists to markers at underarm. Stuff sleeves and leave armholes open. Sew arms to doll at either side, sewing through tunic to body. Place cuffs around wrists and sew up row ends. Sew cast-off stitches to wrists all the way round.

### Features

Work features as for Jack's Mother on page 46.

### Hair and crown

Make up hair as for Jack's Mother on page 46. With right side of knitting outside, bring cast-on and cast-off stitches of crown together and oversew. Curve crown, pin to head and sew in place.

### Cloak collar, cloak and brooch

Place cloak collar around neck and join beneath chin. Sew cast-on stitches of collar to neck. Sew cast-off stitches of cloak to back of neck beneath collar. Sew brooch to centre front of collar beneath chin.

# How to make Courtier

## Shoes, legs, body and head

### Right leg

Beg at sole of shoe, using the thumb method and N, cast on 10 sts.

Place a marker on cast-on edge between the 4th and 5th st of the sts just cast on.

**Row 1 (WS):** Purl.

**Row 2:** K1, (m1, k1) to end (19 sts).

**Rows 3 to 5:** Beg with a p row, work 3 rows in st-st.

### Shape shoe

**Row 6:** K1, (k2tog) 7 times, k4 (12 sts).

**Rows 7 to 27:** Change to C for leg and beg with a p row, work 21 rows in st-st. Break yarn and set aside.

### Left leg

Beg at sole of shoe, using the thumb method and N, cast on 10 sts.

Place a marker on cast-on edge between the 6th and 7th st of the sts just cast on.

**Row 1 (WS):** Purl.

**Row 2:** K1, (m1, k1) to end (19 sts).

**Rows 3 to 5:** Beg with a p row, work 3 rows in st-st.

### Shape shoe

**Row 6:** K4, (k2tog) 7 times, k1 (12 sts).

**Rows 7 to 27:** Change to C for leg and beg with a p row, work 21 rows in st-st.

### Join legs

**Row 28:** Change to A for lower body and k across sts of left leg, and then with the same yarn cont k across sts of right leg (24 sts).

**Rows 29 to 35:** Beg with a p row, work 7 rows in st-st.

**Rows 36 to 49:** Change to Q for upper body and work 14 rows in st-st.

**Rows 50 and 51:** Change to B for head and work 2 rows in st-st.

**Row 52:** K3, (m1, k6) 3 times, m1, k3 (28 sts).

**Rows 53 to 59:** Beg with a p row, work 7 rows in st-st.

### Shape top of head

**Row 60:** (K2tog, k2) to end (21 sts).

**Row 61 and foll alt row:** Purl.

**Row 62:** (K2tog, k1) to end (14 sts).

**Row 64:** (K2tog) to end (7 sts).

Thread yarn through sts on needle and leave loose.

## Breeches

Make breeches as for Jack on page 40, using G.

## Tunic

Beg at lower edge, using the thumb method and H, cast on 44 sts and beg in g-st, RS facing to beg.

**Rows 1 and 2:** Work 2 rows in g-st.

**Rows 3 to 8:** Change to Q and beg with a k row, work 6 rows in st-st.

**Row 9:** K4, (k2tog, k2) 4 times, k6, (k2tog, k2) 4 times, k2 (36 sts).

**Rows 10 to 22:** Beg with a p row, work 13 rows in st-st.

**Row 23:** K3, (k2tog) 6 times, k6, (k2tog) 6 times, k3 (24 sts).

Cast off pwise.

## Sleeves and hands

Make sleeves and hands as for Jack on page 41, using Q for sleeves and B for hands.

## Cuffs

Using the thumb method and H, cast on
16 sts and work in g-st, RS facing to beg.
**Rows 1 and 2:** Work 2 rows in g-st.
**Row 3:** K1, k2tog, (k2, k2tog) to last st,
k1 (12 sts).
Cast off in g-st.

## Collar

Beg at lower edge, using the thumb
method and H, cast on 24 sts and work
in g-st.
**Row 1 (RS):** K4, turn.
**Row 2:** S1k, k to end.
**Row 3:** K6, turn.
**Row 4:** S1k, k to end.
**Row 5:** K across all sts.
**Rows 6 to 9:** Rep rows 1 to 4 once.
Cast off in g-st.

## Hair

Make hair as for Jack on page 42, using R.

## Cushion

Using the thumb method and G, cast on
12 sts, WS facing to beg.
**Rows 1 to 29:** Beg with a p row, work
29 rows in st-st.
Cast off.

## Glass slipper

Using the thumb method and S, cast on
9 sts, WS facing to beg.
**Row 1 and foll 2 alt rows:** Purl.
**Row 2:** K1, (m1, k1) to end (17 sts).
**Row 4:** K4, (k2tog) twice, k1, (k2tog)
twice, k4 (13 sts).
**Row 6:** K5, k3tog, k5 (11 sts).
Cast off kwise.

# Making up Courtier

## Shoes, legs, body and head

Sew up row ends of shoes, and with
markers at tips of toes, oversew cast-
on stitches; leg seam will be ¼in (6mm)
on inside edge of heel. Place a ball of
stuffing into toe of each shoe, pushing
stuffing in with tweezers or tip of scissors.
Sew up row ends of legs and sew round
crotch. Stuff legs, pushing stuffing in with
tweezers or tip of scissors. Sew up row
ends of body, up to halfway up head.
Stuff body and head and pull stitches on
thread tight, fasten off and finish sewing
up row ends. To shape neck, take a double
length of yarn to match upper body and
sew a running stitch round last row of
upper body, sewing in and out of every
half stitch. Pull tight, knot yarn and sew
ends into neck.

## Breeches

Make up as for Jack on Page 43.

## Tunic

Place tunic around doll and sew up row
ends at centre back. Sew cast-off stitches
of tunic to neck all the way round.

## Sleeves and hands

Make up sleeves and hands as for Jack
on page 43, sewing arms forwards to
carry cushion.

## Cuffs

Place cuffs around wrists and oversew row
ends. Sew lower edge of cuffs to wrists all
the way round.

## Collar

Place collar around neck and join beneath
chin. Sew points of collar to chest and
cast-off stitches to neck all the way round.

## Features and hair

Work features and make up hair as for
Jack on page 43.

## Cushion and glass slipper

Bring cast-on and cast-off stitches of
cushion together and sew up. Sew up one
set of row ends and stuff and sew up other
set of row ends. Using gold, embroider a
stem stitch line around outside edge of
cushion. Fold cast-on stitches of slipper in
half and oversew. Oversew row ends and
sew glass slipper to cushion. Sew cushion
to hands of Courtier.

At the very bottom of the ocean stood the Sea King's castle. He lived there with his five mermaid daughters. Sirenetta was the youngest and loveliest and had the most beautiful voice. One day, while swimming near the surface, she saw a young man fall from his ship...

# THE LITTLE MERMAID

# Information you'll need

### Finished size
Mermaid measures 10in (25cm) high

### Materials
**Any DK (US: light worsted) yarn**
**Note:** amounts are approximate
15g pale pink (A)
15g aqua blue (B)
5g purple (C)
Oddments of black, red and pale pink for
embroidery, and 10g bright yellow for hair
1 pair of 3.25mm (UK10:US3) needles
Knitters' blunt-ended pins and a needle
for sewing up
Tweezers for stuffing small parts (optional)
Acrylic toy stuffing
Red pencil for shading cheeks

### Tension
26 sts x 34 rows measure 4in (10cm)
square over st-st using 3.25mm needles
and DK yarn before stuffing.

### Working instructions
Sew up all row-end seams on right side
using mattress stitch, unless otherwise
stated; a one-stitch seam allowance has
been allowed for this.

## How to make The Little Mermaid

### Head and body

Beg at crown of head, using the thumb method and A, cast on 8 sts, WS facing to beg.

**Row 1 and foll 3 alt rows:** Purl.
**Row 2:** K1, (m1, k1) to end (15 sts).
**Row 4:** K1, (m1, k2) to end (22 sts).
**Row 6:** K1, (m1, k3) to end (29 sts).
**Row 8:** K1, (m1, k4) to end (36 sts).
**Rows 9 to 23:** Beg with a p row, work 15 rows in st-st.
Place a marker on last row for the neck gathering.
**Rows 24 to 41:** Work 18 rows in st-st.
Change to B and dec:
**Row 42:** K1, (k2tog, k5) to end (31 sts).
**Row 43:** K1, (p1, k1) to end (this row will be referred to as moss-st and is repeated).
**Rows 44 to 55:** Work 12 rows in moss-st.
**Row 56:** Moss-st 6, k3tog, moss-st 13, k3tog, moss-st 6 (27 sts).
**Rows 57 to 65:** Work 9 rows in moss-st.
**Row 66:** Moss-st 6, k3tog, moss-st 9, k3tog, moss-st 6 (23 sts).
**Rows 67 to 73:** Work 7 rows in moss-st.
**Row 74:** Moss-st 4, k3tog, moss-st 9, k3tog, moss-st 4 (19 sts).
**Rows 75 to 81:** Work 7 rows in moss-st.
**Row 82:** Moss-st 4, k3tog, moss-st 5, k3tog, moss-st 4 (15 sts).
**Rows 83 to 85:** Work 3 rows in moss-st.
**Row 86:** Moss-st 2, k3tog, moss-st 5, k3tog, moss-st 2 (11 sts).
**Rows 87 and 88:** Work 2 rows in moss-st, ending with a RS row.
Cast off in moss-st.

### Tail (make 2 pieces)

Using the thumb method and B, cast on 7 sts.

**Row 1 (WS):** Purl.
**Row 2:** K1, (m1, k1) to end (13 sts).
**Row 3:** Purl.
**Row 4:** K1, (p1, k1) to end.
**Row 5:** P1, (k1, p1) to end.
**Rows 6 to 15:** Rep rows 4 and 5, 5 times more.
**Row 16:** K1, (k2tog) to end (7 sts).
**Row 17:** P1, (p2tog, p1) twice (5 sts).
Thread yarn through sts on needle, pull tight and secure by threading yarn a second time through sts.

## Bikini top
### Cups (make 2)
Using the thumb method and C, cast on 4 sts.

**Row 1 (WS):** Purl.

**Row 2:** K1, (m1, k1) to end (7 sts).

**Rows 3 to 5:** Beg with a p row, work 3 rows in st-st.

**Row 6:** K1, (k2tog, k1) twice (5 sts).

**Row 7:** Purl.

**Row 8:** K2tog, k1, k2tog (3 sts).
Thread yarn through sts on needle, pull tight and secure by threading yarn a second time through sts.

### Strap
Using the thumb method and C, cast on 28 sts, RS facing to beg.
Cast off pwise.

## Arms (make 2)
Beg at top edge, using the thumb method and A, cast on 8 sts.

**Row 1 (WS):** Purl.

**Row 2:** K1, (m1, k2) 3 times, m1, k1 (12 sts).

**Rows 3 to 19:** Beg with a p row, work 17 rows in st-st.
Place a marker on last row for the wrist gathering.

**Rows 20 to 25:** Work 6 rows in st-st.

**Row 26:** (K2tog) to end (6 sts).
Thread yarn through sts on needle, pull tight and secure by threading yarn a second time through sts.

# Making up

### Head and body

Gather round cast-on stitches, pull tight and secure. Sew up row ends of body and head leaving a gap, stuff and sew up gap. To shape neck, take a double length of pale pink yarn and sew a running stitch around row with marker at neck, sewing in and out of every half stitch. Pull tight and knot yarn and sew ends into neck.

### Tail

Sew up row ends of both pieces of tail from tip to ½in (13mm) before top edge, stuff and sew up remainder of row ends. Place both pieces of tail side by side and sew top edge together. Sew tail to lower edge of mermaid.

### Bikini top

Place cups together and oversew cast-on stitches of both pieces. Sew cups to mermaid at centre front, sewing around outside edge. Sew on strap, taking strap from one side, around back and sew to other side, using back stitch down centre of strap.

### Arms

Gather round cast-on stitches of both arms, pull tight and secure. Sew up row ends of arms and hands leaving a gap, stuff and sew up gap. Sew arms to Little Mermaid, sewing top of arm to 4th row below neck.

## Features and hair

Mark position of eyes with two pins on 8th row above neck with three clear knitted stitches in between. Embroider eyes with a double length of black yarn and work a vertical chain stitch for each eye, starting at marked position and ending on row above. Embroider mouth in red on the 4th and 5th rows below eyes, making a shallow 'v' shape across three stitches. Embroider nose in pink at centre front on row below eyes, making a bundle of five horizontal stitches over one stitch (see page 171 for how to begin and fasten off the embroidery invisibly). Shade cheeks with a red pencil. To make hair, cut approx 60 strands of yellow, each strand 15in (38cm) long. Take a long piece of yarn and anchor one end to 6th row above eyes at centre front and sew from forehead, across top of head and down to ½in (13mm) above neck at back using back stitch, and enclose three cut strands of yarn into every stitch. Allow hair to fall neatly and sew from one side around back of head to the other side, using back stitch, sewing through hair to head. Trim ends of hair to ½in (13mm) below waist.

A little red hen lived in a farmyard along with a lamb, a cat and a pig. One sunny spring morning, the hen was scratching around the farmyard when she found some grains of wheat. She asked if the other animals would help her plant the grains, but they refused...

# THE LITTLE RED HEN

# Information you'll need

### Finished size
Little Red Hen measures 9½in (24cm) high

### Materials
**Any DK (US: light worsted) yarn**
**Note:** amounts are approximate
40g red (A)
5g brown (B)
5g gold (C)
Oddment of black for embroidery
1 pair of 3.25mm (UK10:US3) needles
Knitters' blunt-ended pins and a needle
for sewing up
Tweezers for stuffing small parts (optional)
Acrylic toy stuffing

### Tension
26 sts x 34 rows measure 4in (10cm)
square over st-st using 3.25mm needles
and DK yarn before stuffing.

### Working instructions
Sew up all row-end seams on right side
using mattress stitch, unless otherwise
stated; a one-stitch seam allowance has
been allowed for this.

# How to make Little Red Hen

## Body

### Right half

Beg at lower edge, using the thumb method and A, cast on 50 sts.

**Row 1 (WS):** Purl.
**Row 2:** K40, turn.
**Row 3:** S1p, p30, turn.
**Row 4:** S1k, k to end.
**Row 5:** Purl.
**Row 6:** (K2tog, k8) to end (45 sts).

Join on B and work in A and B in stripes, carrying yarn loosely up side of work.

**Rows 7 and 8:** Using B, p 2 rows.
**Row 9:** Change to A and p 1 row.
**Row 10:** K36, turn.
**Row 11:** S1p, p26, turn.
**Row 12:** S1k, k to end.
**Row 13:** Purl.
**Row 14:** (K2tog, k7) to end (40 sts).
**Rows 15 and 16:** Using B, p 2 rows.
**Row 17:** Change to A and p 1 row.
**Row 18:** K32, turn.
**Row 19:** S1p, p22, turn.
**Row 20:** S1k, k to end.
**Row 21:** Purl.
**Row 22:** (K2tog, k6) to end (35 sts).
**Rows 23 and 24:** Using B, p 2 rows.
**Row 25:** Change to A and p 1 row.
**Row 26:** K28, turn.
**Row 27:** S1p, p18, turn.
**Row 28:** S1k, k to end.
**Row 29:** Purl.
**Row 30:** (K2tog, k5) to end (30 sts).
**Rows 31 and 32:** Using B, p 2 rows.
**Row 33:** Change to A and p 1 row.
**Row 34:** K24, turn.
**Row 35:** S1p, p14, turn.
**Row 36:** S1k, k to end.
**Row 37:** Purl.
**Row 38:** (K2tog, k3) to end (24 sts).
**Rows 39 and 40:** Using B, p 2 rows.
**Rows 41 to 43:** Change to A and beg with a p row, work 3 rows in st-st.
**Row 44:** (K2tog, k2) to end (18 sts).
Cast off pwise.

### Left half

Beg at lower edge, using the thumb method and A, cast on 50 sts.
**Row 1 (WS):** Purl.
**Row 2:** K41, turn.
**Row 3:** S1p, p30, turn.
**Row 4:** S1k, k to end.
**Row 5:** Purl.
**Row 6:** (K8, k2tog) to end (45 sts).
Join in B and work in A and B in stripes, carrying yarn loosely up side of work.

**Rows 7 and 8:** Using B, p 2 rows.
**Row 9:** Change to A and p 1 row.
**Row 10:** K36, turn.
**Row 11:** S1p, p26, turn.
**Row 12:** S1k, k to end.
**Row 13:** Purl.
**Row 14:** (K7, k2tog) to end (40 sts).
**Rows 15 and 16:** Using B, p 2 rows.
**Row 17:** Change to A and p 1 row.
**Row 18:** K31, turn.
**Row 19:** S1p, p22, turn.
**Row 20:** S1k, k to end.
**Row 21:** Purl.
**Row 22:** (K6, k2tog) to end (35 sts).
**Rows 23 and 24:** Using B, p 2 rows.
**Row 25:** Change to A and p 1 row.
**Row 26:** K26, turn.
**Row 27:** S1p, p18, turn.
**Row 28:** S1k, k to end.
**Row 29:** Purl.
**Row 30:** (K5, k2tog) to end (30 sts).
**Rows 31 and 32:** Using B, p 2 rows.
**Row 33:** Change to A and p 1 row.
**Row 34:** K21, turn.
**Row 35:** S1p, p14, turn.
**Row 36:** S1k, k to end.
**Row 37:** Purl.
**Row 38:** (K3, k2tog) to end (24 sts).
**Rows 39 and 40:** Using B, p 2 rows.
**Rows 41 to 43:** Change to A and beg with a p row, work 3 rows in st-st.
**Row 44:** (K2, k2tog) to end (18 sts).
Cast off pwise.

## Head

Using the thumb method and A, cast on 40 sts, WS facing to beg.

**Rows 1 to 13:** Beg with a p row, work 13 rows in st-st.

**Row 14:** (K1, k2tog, k14, k2tog tbl, k1) twice (36 sts).

**Row 15 and foll 4 alt rows:** Purl.

**Row 16:** (K1, k2tog, k12, k2tog tbl, k1) twice (32 sts).

**Row 18:** (K1, k2tog, k10, k2tog tbl, k1) twice (28 sts).

**Row 20:** (K1, k2tog, k8, k2tog tbl, k1) twice (24 sts).

**Row 22:** (K1, k2tog, k6, k2tog tbl, k1) twice (20 sts).

**Row 24:** (K2tog) to end (10 sts).

Thread yarn through sts on needle, pull tight and secure by threading yarn a second time through sts.

## Tail

Using the thumb method and A, cast on 40 sts and work in g-st, RS facing to beg.

**Rows 1 to 8:** Work 8 rows in g-st.

**Shape tail**

**Row 9:** K6, turn and work on these 6 sts.

**Rows 10 to 18:** Work 9 rows in g-st.

**Row 19 (RS):** K2tog, k2, k2tog (4 sts).

**Row 20:** Knit.

Thread yarn through sts on needle, pull tight and secure by threading yarn a second time through sts.

**Row 21:** With RS facing, rejoin yarn to rem sts and k8, turn and work on these 8 sts.

**Rows 22 to 32:** Work 11 rows in g-st.

**Row 33:** K2tog, k4, k2tog (6 sts).

**Row 34:** Knit.

**Row 35:** K2tog, k2, k2tog (4 sts).

**Row 36:** Knit.

Thread yarn through sts on needle, pull tight and secure by threading yarn a second time through sts.

**Row 37:** With RS facing, rejoin yarn to rem sts and k12, turn and work on these 12 sts.

**Rows 38 to 46:** Work 9 rows in g-st.

**Row 47:** (K2tog, k2, k2tog) twice (8 sts).

**Row 48:** Knit.

Thread yarn through sts on needle, pull tight and secure by threading yarn a second time through sts.

**Row 49:** With RS facing, rejoin yarn to rem sts and k8, turn and work on these 8 sts.

**Rows 50 to 64:** Rep rows 22 to 36 once (4 sts).

Thread yarn through sts on needle, pull tight and secure by threading yarn a second time through sts.

**Row 65:** With RS facing, rejoin yarn to rem sts and k6 (6 sts).

**Rows 66 to 76:** Rep rows 10 to 20 once (4 sts).

Thread yarn through sts on needle, pull tight and secure by threading yarn a second time through sts.

## Comb (make 2 pieces)

Using the thumb method and A, cast on 10 sts, WS facing to beg.

**Rows 1 to 3:** Beg with a p row, work 3 rows in st-st.

**Row 4:** (K1, m1) twice, (k2, m1) 3 times, k1, m1, k1 (16 sts).

**Row 5:** P5, turn and work on these 5 sts.

**Row 6:** Knit.

**Row 7:** Purl.

**Row 8:** K2tog, k1, k2tog (3 sts).

Thread yarn through sts on needle, pull tight and secure by threading yarn a second time through sts.

**Row 9:** Rejoin yarn to rem sts and p6, turn and work on these 6 sts.

**Rows 10 to 13:** Beg with a k row, work 4 rows in st-st.

**Row 14:** K1, (k2tog) twice, k1 (4 sts).

Thread yarn through sts on needle, pull tight and secure by threading yarn a second time through sts.

**Row 15:** Rejoin yarn to rem sts and p5, turn and work on these 5 sts.

**Row 16:** Knit.

**Row 17:** Purl.

**Row 18:** K2tog, k1, k2tog (3 sts).

Thread yarn through sts on needle, pull tight and secure by threading yarn a second time through sts.

## Beak

Using the thumb method and C, cast on 13 sts.

**Row 1 (WS):** Purl.

**Row 2:** K2tog, k to last 2 sts, k2tog (11 sts).

**Rows 3 to 8:** Rep rows 1 and 2, 3 times more (5 sts).

Thread yarn through sts on needle, pull tight and secure by threading yarn a second time through sts.

## Crop (make 2 pieces)

Beg at top edge, using the thumb method and A, cast on 3 sts, WS facing to beg.

**Row 1 and foll alt row:** Purl.

**Row 2:** K1, m1, k1, m1, k1 (5 sts).

**Row 4:** K2, m1, k1, m1, k2 (7 sts).

**Rows 5 to 7:** Beg with a p row, work 3 rows in st-st.

**Row 8:** K1, k2tog, k1, k2tog, k1 (5 sts).

Thread yarn through sts on needle, pull tight and secure by threading yarn a second time through sts.

## Eye pieces (make 2)

Using the thumb method and A, cast on 6 sts and work in g-st.

**Row 1 (RS):** Knit.

**Row 2:** K1, m1, k4, m1, k1 (8 sts).

**Rows 3 and 4:** Work 2 rows in g-st.

**Row 5:** K2, (k2tog) twice, k2 (6 sts).

**Row 6:** Knit.

**Row 7:** K1, (k2tog) twice, k1 (4 sts). Cast off in g-st.

## Wings (make 2)

Using the thumb method and A, cast on 8 sts and work in g-st.

**Row 1 (RS):** Knit.

**Row 2:** K1, m1, k to last st m1, k1 (10 sts).

**Rows 3 to 8:** Rep rows 1 and 2, 3 times more (16 sts).

**Rows 9 to 18:** Work 10 rows in g-st.

**Row 19:** K1, k2tog, k to last 3 sts, k2tog, k1 (14 sts).

**Rows 20 to 22:** Work 3 rows in g-st.

**Rows 23 to 34:** Rep rows 19 to 22, 3 times more (8 sts).

**Row 35:** As row 19 (6 sts).

**Row 36:** Knit.

**Row 37:** K1, (k2tog) twice, k1 (4 sts).

**Row 38:** Knit.

Thread yarn through sts on needle, pull tight and secure by threading yarn a second time through sts.

## Feet (make 4 pieces)

Using the thumb method and C, cast on 25 sts and work in g-st.

**Row 1 (RS):** K3, (k3tog, k5) twice, k3tog, k3 (19 sts).

**Row 2 and foll alt row:** Knit.

**Row 3:** K2, (k3tog, k3) twice, k3tog, k2 (13 sts).

**Row 5:** K1, (k3tog, k1) 3 times (7 sts).

**Rows 6 to 10:** Work 5 rows in g-st.

**Row 11:** K2, k3tog, k2 (5 sts).

**Rows 12 to 16:** Work 5 rows in g-st.

**Row 17:** K1, k3tog, k1 (3 sts).

**Row 18:** Knit.

Thread yarn through sts on needle, pull tight and secure by threading yarn a second time through sts.

## Legs (make 2)

Using the thumb method and A, cast on 10 sts, WS facing to beg.

**Rows 1 to 7:** Beg with a p row, work 7 rows in st-st. Cast off.

## Tops of legs (make 2)

Using the thumb method and A, cast on 16 sts, WS facing to beg.

**Rows 1 to 5:** Beg with a p row, work 5 rows in st-st.

**Rows 6 and 7:** P 2 rows to mark fold line.

**Row 8:** (K2tog) to end (8 sts).

Thread yarn through sts on needle, pull tight and secure by threading yarn a second time through sts.

# Making up

### Body, head and tail

Sew up cast-off stitches of two pieces of body and open piece out flat. With right sides together, pin and sew cast-on stitches of head to front of neck opening by sewing back and forth on wrong side one stitch in from the edge. Pin and sew tail to back opening likewise. Sew up row ends of head and then sew up row ends of tail by oversewing. Stuff head and tail firmly, and then stuff body, keeping it flat. Sew up cast-on stitches at lower edge.

### Comb

Place two pieces of comb together matching all edges and sew up around shaped edge from one side to the other. Stuff comb, pushing stuffing into top with tweezers or tip of scissors. Sew comb to top of head.

### Beak

Sew up row ends of beak from tip to base and stuff, pushing stuffing in with tweezers or tip of scissors. Sew cast-on stitches of beak to head at centre front.

### Crop

Sew up row ends of lower half of each piece of crop and stuff lower half with a tiny ball of stuffing, pushing stuffing in with tweezers or tip of scissors. Finish sewing up row ends of both pieces, place them side by side and sew together. Sew crop to Hen below beak at centre front.

### Eye pieces

Sew eye pieces to head using back stitch around outside edge.

### Wings

Pin and sew wings to body using back stitch around outside edge.

### Feet

Place two pieces of feet together matching all edges and oversew cast-on stitches. Place a tiny ball of stuffing into each toe, pushing stuffing in with tweezers or tip of scissors. Oversew row ends leaving a gap, stuff foot and sew up gap. Repeat for other foot.

### Legs

Sew up row ends of each leg leaving top and bottom open, and stuff firmly. Sew one end of each leg to the top of each foot.

### Tops of legs

Sew up row ends of tops of legs and stuff. Sew lower edge of tops of legs to top of legs and feet and pin and sew tops of legs to underneath of body.

### Features

Embroider eyes in black on eye pieces: make a chain stitch for each eye then another chain stitch on top of first chain stitch (see page 171 for how to begin and fasten off the embroidery invisibly).

Once upon a time there were three little pigs. The first pig quickly built his house from straw. The second pig quickly built his house from sticks. The third pig spent all day building his house from bricks. Watching close by was a big, bad wolf...

# THREE LITTLE PIGS

# Information you'll need

### Finished sizes
Pigs measure 8½in (22cm) high
Straw measures 2¾in (7cm) long
Sticks measure 4½in (11cm) long
Bricks measure 2in (5cm) high
Wolf measures 6¼in (16cm) high

### Materials
**Any DK (US: light worsted) yarn**
**Note:** amounts are approximate
125g piggy pink (A)
15g red (B)
15g green (C)
15g blue (D)
5g lemon (E)
5g brown (F)
5g terracotta (G)
10g beige (H)
15g dark brown (I)
Oddments of black, grey and beige for
embroidery
1 pair of 3.25mm (UK10:US3) needles and
a spare needle of the same size
A stitch holder
Knitters' blunt-ended pins and a needle for
sewing up
Tweezers for stuffing small parts (optional)
Acrylic toy stuffing
5 drinking straws

### Tension
26 sts x 34 rows measure 4in (10cm)
square over st-st using 3.25mm needles
and DK yarn before stuffing.

### Working instructions
Sew up all row-end seams on right side
using mattress stitch, unless otherwise
stated; a one-stitch seam allowance has
been allowed for this.

# How to make Pig

## (Make 3 Pigs)

### Body

Beg at lower edge, using the thumb method and A, cast on 9 sts, WS facing to beg.

**Row 1 and foll 5 alt rows:** Purl.
**Row 2:** K1, (m1, k1) to end (17 sts).
**Row 4:** K1, (m1, k2) to end (25 sts).
**Row 6:** K1, (m1, k3) to end (33 sts).
**Row 8:** K1, (m1, k4) to end (41 sts).
**Row 10:** K1, (m1, k5) to end (49 sts).
**Row 12:** K1, (m1, k6) to end (57 sts).
**Rows 13 to 27:** Beg with a p row, work 15 rows in st-st.

### Shape body

**Row 28:** K1, (k2tog, k5) to end (49 sts).
**Rows 29 to 33:** Beg with a p row work 5 rows in st-st.
**Row 34:** K1, (k2tog, k4) to end (41 sts).
**Rows 35 to 37:** Beg with a p row, work 3 rows in st-st.
**Row 38:** K1, (k2tog, k3) to end (33 sts).
Cast off pwise.

### Head

Beg at lower edge, using the thumb method and A, cast on 9 sts, WS facing to beg.
**Row 1 and foll 4 alt rows:** Purl.

**Row 2:** K1, (m1, k1) to end (17 sts).
**Row 4:** K1, (m1, k2) to end (25 sts).
**Row 6:** K1, (m1, k3) to end (33 sts).
**Row 8:** K1, (m1, k4) to end (41 sts).
**Row 10:** K1, (m1, k5) to end (49 sts).
**Rows 11 to 25:** Beg with a p row, work 15 rows in st-st.

### Shape head

**Row 26:** K1, (k2tog, k4) to end (41 sts).
**Row 27:** Purl.
**Row 28:** K1, (k2tog, k3) to end (33 sts).
**Rows 29 to 33:** Beg with a p row, work 5 rows in st-st.
**Row 34:** K1, (k2tog, k2) to end (25 sts).
**Row 35 and foll alt row:** Purl.
**Row 36:** K1, (k2tog, k1) to end (17 sts).
**Row 38:** K1, (k2tog) to end (9 sts).
Thread yarn through sts on needle, pull tight and secure by threading yarn a second time through sts.

### Legs (make 2)

Beg at top edge, using the thumb method and A, cast on 22 sts.
**Row 1 (WS):** Purl.
**Row 2:** K16, turn.
**Row 3:** S1p, p9, turn.
**Row 4:** S1k, k to end.
**Rows 5 to 9:** Beg with a p row, work 5 rows in st-st.
**Row 10:** K1, k2tog, k to last 3 sts, k2tog, k1 (20 sts).
**Rows 11 to 16:** Rep rows 5 to 10 once (18 sts).
**Rows 17 to 19:** Beg with a p row, work 3 rows in st-st.
**Row 20:** (K2tog, k5, k2tog) twice (14 sts).
Cast off pwise.

## Arms (make 2)

Using the thumb method and A, cast on 6 sts.

**Row 1 (WS):** Purl.

**Row 2:** (K1, m1) twice, k2, (m1, k1) twice (10 sts).

**Row 3:** Purl.

**Row 4:** K1, m1, k to last st m1, k1 (12 sts).

**Rows 5 to 12:** Rep rows 3 and 4, 4 times more (20 sts).

Place a marker on first and last st of the last row.

**Rows 13 to 21:** Beg with a p row, work 9 rows in st-st.

**Row 22:** (K2tog, k2) to end (15 sts).

**Row 23:** Purl.

**Row 24:** (K2tog, k1) to end (10 sts). Thread yarn through sts on needle, pull tight and secure by threading yarn a second time through sts.

## Snout

Beg at face edge, using the thumb method and A, cast on 19 sts, WS facing to beg.

**Rows 1 to 5:** Beg with a p row, work 5 rows in st-st.

**Rows 6 and 7:** P 1 row then k 1 row for fold line.

**Row 8:** K 1 row.

**Row 9:** P1, (p2tog, p1) to end (13 sts).

**Row 10:** K1, (k2tog, k1) to end (9 sts). Thread yarn through sts on needle, pull tight and secure by threading yarn a second time through sts.

## Ears (make 2)

Beg at base, using the thumb method and A, cast on 14 sts.

**Row 1 (WS):** Purl.

**Row 2:** (K2, m1, k3, m1, k2) twice (18 sts).

**Rows 3 to 9:** Beg with a p row, work 7 rows in st-st.

**Row 10:** K3, k2tog, k8, k2tog, k3 (16 sts).

**Row 11 and foll 3 alt rows:** Purl.

**Row 12:** K3, k2tog, k6, k2tog, k3 (14 sts).

**Row 14:** K2, k3tog, k4, k3tog, k2 (10 sts).

**Row 16:** K1, k3tog, k2, k3tog, k1 (6 sts).

**Row 18:** K1, (k2tog) twice, k1 (4 sts). Thread yarn through sts on needle, pull tight and secure by threading yarn a second time through sts.

## Dungarees (make one pair in each of B, C and D)

### Back

### First leg

Beg at lower edge, using the thumb method and B, C or D, cast on 15 sts and beg in g-st, RS facing to beg.

**Rows 1 and 2:** Work 2 rows in g-st.

**Rows 3 to 6:** Beg with a k row, work 4 rows in st-st.

Break yarn and set aside.

### Second leg

Work as first leg but do not break yarn.

### Join legs

**Row 7:** With RS facing, k across sts of second leg, turn, and using the knitting-on method, cast on 5 sts, turn, and with the same yarn cont k across sts of first leg (35 sts).

**Rows 8 to 28:** Beg with a p row, work 21 rows in st-st.

**Rows 29 to 31:** Work 3 rows in g-st, ending with a RS row. ＊＊

Cast off in g-st.

### Front

Work as back from beg to ＊＊.

### Cont as foll:

**Row 32:** Cast off 9 sts kwise, k16 (17 sts now on RH needle), cast off rem 9 sts (17 sts).

**Row 33:** Break yarn and rejoin to rem sts with RS facing and k 1 row.

**Row 34:** K2, p to last 2 sts, k2.

**Row 35:** K2, k2tog, k to last 4 sts, k2tog, k2 (15 sts).

**Row 36:** As row 34.

**Row 37:** Knit.

**Row 38:** As row 34.

**Rows 39 to 42:** Rep rows 35 to 38 (13 sts).

**Rows 43 to 45:** Work 3 rows in g-st, ending with a RS row.

Cast off in g-st.

### Straps (make 2)

Using the thumb method and colour to match dungarees, cast on 30 sts.

**Row 1 (RS):** Knit.

Cast off kwise.

### Tail

Using the thumb method and A, cast on 20 sts.

**Row 1 (RS):** Knit.

Cast off kwise.

# Making up Pig

## Body
Sew up row ends of body from lower edge to neck and leave neck open. Stuff body.

## Head
Sew up row ends of head leaving a gap, stuff head and sew up gap. Pin and sew head to body by taking a horizontal stitch from head, then a horizontal stitch from body and do this alternately all the way round, leaving a gap. Add more stuffing to neck and sew up gap.

## Legs
Fold cast-off stitches of legs in half and sew up. Sew up row ends of legs and stuff. Pin and sew legs centrally to underneath with a ¾in (2cm) gap between legs at crotch.

## Arms
Sew up row ends of arms from lower edge to markers and stuff arms. Sew arms to body at either side.

## Snout
Sew up row ends of snout and stuff. Pin and sew snout centrally to face leaving two clear knitted rows between neck and snout.

## Features
Mark position of eyes with two pins on row above snout with five clear knitted stitches in between. Embroider a chain stitch in black for each eye beginning at marked position and finishing on row above and then a second chain stitch on top of first. Embroider nostrils in grey, making a single chain stitch. Using picture

as a guide, embroider mouth in grey using straight stitches (see page 171 for how to begin and fasten off the embroidery invisibly).

## Ears
Sew up row ends of ears and with this seam at centre of underneath edge, oversew cast-on stitches. Sew cast-on stitches of ears to back of head, bend ears forwards and sew tips in place.

## Dungarees and straps
Place front and back of dungarees together, matching all edges, and sew up row ends of inside legs and across crotch. Sew up outside edge of front and back and place dungarees on Pig. Sew one end of each strap to top of bib, take straps across shoulders, cross them over at the back and sew ends to waist of dungarees at back.

## Tail
Tie a loose knot in tail and sew through this knot to secure. Sew tail to dungarees at back, sewing through dungarees to Pig.

## Making up Straw, Sticks and Bricks

### Straw

Using lemon, cut a bundle of 2½in (6cm) lengths of yarn; the bundle will be 1½in (4cm) in diameter. Place tie around middle of bundle and oversew row ends. Sew back and forth through centre of bundle to secure strands.

### Sticks

Cut five straws to a length of 3¼in (8cm). Place knitting around straws and oversew row ends along length. Gather round cast-on stitches and cast-off stitches, pull tight and secure. Using picture as a guide, sew Sticks together in a bundle.

### Bricks

Sew up cast-on and cast-off stitches of top, bottom, front and back and sew one end piece to make a box shape. Stuff and sew on last end piece to make a cube. Using picture as a guide, embroider Bricks in beige (see page 171 for how to begin and fasten off the embroidery invisibly).

## How to make Straw, Sticks and Bricks

### Straw

**Tie**

Using the thumb method and E, cast on 15 sts, RS facing to beg.
Cast off pwise.

### Sticks (make 5)

Using the thumb method and F, cast on 6 sts and work in rev st-st, RS facing to beg. Beg with a p row, work in rev st-st for 4in (10cm). Cast off in rev st-st.

### Bricks

**Top, bottom, front and back (make 4 pieces)**

Using the thumb method and G, cast on 14 sts, WS facing to beg.

**Rows 1 to 3:** Beg with a p row, work 3 rows in st-st.

**Rows 4 and 5:** Join in H and work 2 rows in g-st.

**Rows 6 to 9:** Carrying yarn loosely up side of work, using G and beg with a k row, work 4 rows in st-st.

**Rows 10 to 15:** Rep rows 4 to 9 once. Cast off in G.

**Ends (make 2 pieces)**

Using the thumb method and G, cast on 10 sts and work rows 1 to 15 as for top, bottom, front and back.

# How to make Wolf

## Body

Beg at base, using the thumb method and I, cast on 9 sts, WS facing to beg.

**Row 1 and foll 3 alt rows:** Purl.
**Row 2:** K1, (m1, k1) to end (17 sts).
**Row 4:** K1, (m1, k2) to end (25 sts).
**Row 6:** K1, (m1, k3) to end (33 sts).
**Row 8:** K1, (m1, k4) to end (41 sts).
**Row 9:** P32, place rem sts onto stitch holder, turn and work on these 32 sts and shape as foll:
**Row 10:** K2tog, k to last 2 sts, k2tog (30 sts).
**Row 11:** Purl.
**Row 12:** As row 10 (28 sts).
**Rows 13 to 37:** Beg with a p row, work 25 rows in st-st.
**Row 38:** K1, m1, k to last st, m1, k1 (30 sts).
**Row 39:** P1, m1, p to last st, m1, p1 (32 sts).
**Rows 40 to 43:** Rep rows 38 and 39 twice more (40 sts).
**Row 44:** K1, (k2tog, k1) to end (27 sts). Cast off pwise.

## Work belly

**Row 45:** With WS facing, rejoin yarn H to rem sts and p to end (9 sts).
**Row 46:** K1, m1, k to last st, m1, k1 (11 sts).
**Row 47:** Purl.
**Row 48:** As row 46 (13 sts).
**Rows 49 to 73:** Beg with a p row, work 25 rows in st-st.
**Row 74:** K2tog, k to last 2 sts, k2tog (11 sts).
**Row 75:** P2tog, p to last 2 sts, p2tog (9 sts).
**Rows 76 and 77:** Rep rows 74 and 75 once (5 sts).
**Row 78:** K2tog, k1, k2tog (3 sts). Cast off pwise.

## Head

Beg at back, using the thumb method and I, cast on 9 sts, WS facing to beg.

**Row 1 and foll 3 alt rows:** Purl.
**Row 2:** K1, (m1, k1) to end (17 sts).
**Row 4:** K1, (m1, k2) to end (25 sts).
**Row 6:** K1, (m1, k3) to end (33 sts).
**Row 8:** K1, (m1, k4) to end (41 sts).
**Rows 9 to 19:** Beg with a p row, work 11 rows in st-st.
**Row 20:** K7, (k2tog, k3) to last 4 sts, k4 (35 sts).

**Row 21 and foll alt row:** Purl.
**Row 22:** K6, (k2tog, k1) 8 times, k5 (27 sts).
**Row 24:** K2, (k2tog, k1) to last st, k1 (19 sts).
**Rows 25 to 35:** Beg with a p row, work 11 rows in st-st.
**Row 36:** K1, (k2tog, k1) to end (13 sts).
**Row 37:** P1, (p2tog, p1) to end (9 sts).
Thread yarn through sts on needle, pull tight and secure by threading yarn a second time through sts.

## Ears (make 2)

Using the thumb method and I, cast on 12 sts, WS facing to beg.

**Rows 1 to 3:** Beg with a p row, work 3 rows in st-st.

**Row 4:** (K2tog, k2, k2tog) twice (8 sts).

**Row 5:** (P2tog) to end (4 sts).

Thread yarn through sts on needle, pull tight and secure by threading yarn a second time through sts.

## Tail

Beg at base, using the thumb method and I, cast on 10 sts, WS facing to beg.

**Rows 1 to 5:** Beg with a p row, work 5 rows in st-st.

**Row 6:** K1, m1, k to last st, m1, k1 (12 sts).

**Rows 7 to 18:** Rep rows 1 to 6 twice more (16 sts).

**Row 19:** Purl.

**Row 20:** K1, m1, k to last st, m1, k1 (18 sts).

**Rows 21 and 22:** Rep rows 19 and 20 once (20 sts).

**Row 23:** Purl.

**Rows 24 to 27:** Change to H and work 4 rows in g-st.

**Row 28:** *K3, (k2tog) twice, k3; rep from * once (16 sts).

**Row 29 and foll alt row:** Purl.

**Row 30:** *K2, (k2tog) twice, k2; rep from * once (12 sts).

**Row 32:** *K1, (k2tog) twice, k1; rep from * once (8 sts).

Thread yarn through sts on needle, pull tight and secure by threading yarn a second time through sts.

## Hind legs (make 2)

Using the thumb method and I, cast on 13 sts.

**Row 1 (WS):** Purl.

**Row 2:** K1, m1, k to last st, m1, k1 (15 sts).

**Rows 3 to 6:** Rep rows 1 and 2 twice more (19 sts).

**Rows 7 to 11:** Beg with a p row, work 5 rows in st-st.

**Shape paw**

**Row 12:** K1, (k2tog, k1) to end (13 sts).

**Row 13:** P1, (p2tog, p1) to end (9 sts).

Thread yarn through sts on needle, pull tight and secure by threading yarn a second time through sts.

## Front legs (make 2)

Beg at top of leg, using the thumb method and I, cast on 11 sts.

**Row 1 (WS):** Purl.

**Row 2:** K1, m1, k to last st, m1, k1 (13 sts).

**Rows 3 to 7:** Beg with a p row, work 5 rows in st-st.

**Rows 8 to 19:** Rep rows 2 to 7 twice more (17 sts).

**Shape paw**

**Row 20:** K2tog, (k1, k2tog) to end (11 sts).

Thread yarn through sts on needle, pull tight and secure by threading yarn a second time through sts.

# Making up Wolf

## Body
Gather round cast-on stitches, pull tight and secure. Sew up base and sew up row ends of belly and body. Leaving neck open, stuff body.

## Head
Gather round cast-on stitches, pull tight and secure. Sew up row ends of snout and stuff. Finish sewing up row ends of head leaving a gap, stuff and sew up gap. Pin and sew head to body, taking a horizontal stitch from head, then a horizontal stitch from body and do this alternately all the way round.

## Hind legs
Sew up row ends of hind legs and stuff, pushing stuffing in with tweezers or tip of scissors. With seam at centre of underneath edge, sew across cast-on stitches of hind legs. Place body on a flat surface, assemble hind legs and sew to front of Wolf.

## Front legs
Sew up row ends of paws and stuff. Finish sewing up row ends, pushing a little stuffing inside as you sew. With seam at centre of inside edge, sew across cast-on stitches and sew front legs to sides of Wolf.

## Ears
Sew up row ends of ears and sew ears to top of head.

## Features
Mark position of eyes with two pins on head with four clear knitted stitches in between. Embroider eyes in black and work a chain stitch for each eye and then a second chain stitch on top of first chain stitch. Using picture as a guide, work straight stitches in black for nose and stem stitch for mouth (see page 171 for how to begin and fasten off the embroidery invisibly).

## Tail
Sew up row ends of wide part of tail and stuff. Finish sewing up row ends, pushing a little stuffing inside as you sew. Sew across cast-on stitches of tail and sew tail to back of Wolf.

Once there was a princess who had a golden ball. One day while playing with the golden ball she accidentally dropped it into a pond. As she was crying, a frog hopped out of the pond and said he could get her ball back but asked for a kiss in return...

# THE FROG PRINCE

# Information you'll need

## Finished sizes

Princess measures 6¾in (16.5cm) high
Golden Ball measures ¾in (2cm) across
Frog measures 6in (15cm) long
Prince measures 8½in (22cm) high

## Materials

**Any DK (US: light worsted) yarn**
**Note:** amounts are approximate
5g white (A)
15g pale pink (B)
10g mustard (C)
5g gold (D)
20g bright green (E)
5g black (F)
5g grey (G)
20g lime green (H)
20g dark green (I)
10g brown (J)
5g lemon (K)
Oddments of black, red, pale pink, dark green and 5g golden cream for embroidery
1 pair of 3.25mm (UK10:US3) needles and a spare needle of the same size
Knitters' blunt-ended pins and a needle for sewing up
Tweezers for stuffing small parts (optional)
Acrylic toy stuffing
Red pencil for shading cheeks
4 chenille sticks

## Tension

26 sts x 34 rows measure 4in (10cm) square over st-st using 3.25mm needles and DK yarn before stuffing.

## Working instructions

Sew up all row-end seams on right side using mattress stitch, unless otherwise stated; a one-stitch seam allowance has been allowed for this.

# How to make Princess and Golden Ball

## Shoes, legs, body and head

### Right leg

Beg at sole of shoe, using the thumb method and A, cast on 10 sts.
Place a marker on cast-on edge between the 4th and 5th st of the sts just cast on.
**Row 1 (WS):** Purl.
**Row 2:** K1, (m1, k1) to end (19 sts).
**Rows 3 to 5:** Beg with a p row, work 3 rows in st-st.
Change to B for leg and shape shoe:
**Row 6:** K1, (k2tog) 7 times, k4 (12 sts).
**Rows 7 to 27:** Beg with a p row, work 21 rows in st-st.
Break yarn and set aside.

### Left leg

Beg at sole of shoe, using the thumb method and A, cast on 10 sts.
Place a marker on cast-on edge between the 6th and 7th st of the sts just cast on.
**Row 1 (WS):** Purl.
**Row 2:** K1, (m1, k1) to end (19 sts).
**Rows 3 to 5:** Beg with a p row, work 3 rows in st-st.
Change to B for leg and shape shoe:
**Row 6:** K4, (k2tog) 7 times, k1 (12 sts).
**Rows 7 to 27:** Beg with a p row, work 21 rows in st-st.

### Join legs

**Row 28:** Change to A for lower body and k across sts of left leg, and then with the same yarn cont k across sts of right leg (24 sts).
**Rows 29 to 35:** Beg with a p row, work 7 rows in st-st.
**Rows 36 to 45:** Change to C for upper body and work 10 rows in st-st.
**Rows 46 to 49:** Change to B for neck and head and work 4 rows in st-st.
Place a marker on last row for the neck gathering.
**Rows 50 and 51:** Work 2 rows in st-st.
**Row 52:** K3, (m1, k6) 3 times, m1, k3 (28 sts).
**Rows 53 to 59:** Beg with a p row, work 7 rows in st-st.

### Shape top of head

**Row 60:** (K2tog, k2) to end (21 sts).
**Row 61 and foll alt row:** Purl.
**Row 62:** (K2tog, k1) to end (14 sts).
**Row 64:** (K2tog) to end (7 sts).
Thread yarn through sts on needle and leave loose.

## Skirt of dress

Beg at lower edge, using the thumb method and D, cast on 50 sts, WS facing to beg.
**Rows 1 and 2:** P 1 row then k 1 row (this part is turned under).
**Picot row:** K2, (yf, k2tog) to end.
**Rows 4 and 5:** K1 row then p 1 row.
**Rows 6 and 7:** Change to A and work 2 rows in g-st.
**Rows 8 to 21:** Change to C and beg with a k row, work 14 rows in st-st.
**Row 22:** (K2tog, k3) to end (40 sts).
**Rows 23 to 25:** Beg with a p row, work 3 rows in st-st.
**Row 26:** (K2tog, k2) to end (30 sts).
Cast off pwise.

## Sash

Using the thumb method and D, cast on 30 sts, RS facing to beg.
Cast off pwise.

## Sleeves and hands (make 2)

Make sleeves and hands as for Jack on page 41, using C for sleeves and B for hands.

## Neckband

Using the thumb method and C, cast on 36 sts, RS facing to beg.
Cast off pwise.

## Crown

Using the thumb method and K, cast on 24 sts, WS facing to beg.
**Picot row:** K2, (yf, k2tog) to end.
**Row 2:** Knit.
Cast off pwise.

## Golden ball

Using the thumb method and D, cast on
6 sts, WS facing to beg.

**Row 1 and foll alt row:** Purl.

**Row 2:** K1, (m1, k1) to end (11 sts).

**Row 4:** K1, (m1, k2) to end (16 sts).

**Rows 5 to 9:** Beg with a p row, work
5 rows in st-st.

**Row 10:** K1, (k2tog, k1) to end (11 sts).

**Row 11:** Purl.

**Row 12:** K1, (k2tog) to end (6 sts).
Thread yarn through sts on needle,
pull tight and secure by threading yarn
a second time through sts.

# Making up Princess and Golden Ball

### Shoes, legs, body and head

Sew up row ends of shoes and ankles and,
with markers at tips of toes, then oversew
cast-on stitches; leg seam will be ¼in
(6mm) on inside edge of heel. Place a ball
of stuffing into toe of each shoe, pushing
stuffing in with tweezers or tip of scissors.
Sew up row ends of legs and sew round
crotch. Stuff legs, pushing stuffing in with
tweezers or tip of scissors. Sew up row
ends of body, up to halfway up head. Stuff
body and head, and pull stitches on thread
tight and fasten off. Finish sewing up row
ends. To shape neck, take a double length
of pale pink and sew a running stitch
round row with marker, sewing in and out
of every half stitch. Pull tight, knot yarn
and sew ends into neck.

### Skirt of dress and sash

Turn hem under and sew in place. Sew
up row ends of skirt of dress and place
on doll. Sew cast-off stitches of skirt of
dress to first row of upper body all the
way round. Place sash around waist and
oversew row ends. Sew sash to doll using
back stitch down centre of sash all the
way round.

### Sleeves and hands

Sew up row ends of hands and place a
small ball of stuffing into hands, pushing
stuffing in with tweezers or tip of scissors.
Sew up sleeves from wrists to markers at
underarm. Stuff arms, pushing stuffing in
with tweezers or tip of scissors and leave
armholes open. Sew arms to doll at either
side, sewing top of arm to second row
below neck.

### Neckband

Place neckband around neck and oversew
row ends. Pin and sew neckband around
top of dress and over shoulders using back
stitch down centre of band.

### Features and hair

Work features as for Jack on page 43.
To make hair, cut approx 45 strands of
golden cream, each strand 10in (25cm)
long. Take a long piece of yarn and anchor
one end to 3rd row above eyes at centre
front and sew from forehead, across top
of head and down to ½in (13mm) above
neck at back using back stitch, and enclose
three cut strands of yarn in every stitch.
Allow hair to fall neatly and sew from one
side around back of head to the other side
using back stitch, sewing through hair to
head. Trim ends of hair to waist.

### Crown

With right side of knitting outside, bring
cast-on and cast-off stitches of crown
together and oversew. Oversew row ends,
pin crown to head and sew in place.

### Golden ball

Gather round cast-on stitches of golden
ball and sew up row ends, leaving a gap.
Stuff and sew up gap.

# How to make Frog

## Body and head

Beg at back, using the thumb method and E, cast on 22 sts, WS facing to beg. Place a marker at the centre of cast-on edge.

**Row 1 and foll 5 alt rows:** Purl.
**Row 2:** (K5, m1, k1, m1, k5) twice (26 sts).
**Row 4:** (K6, m1, k1, m1, k6) twice (30 sts).
**Row 6:** (K7, m1, k1, m1, k7) twice (34 sts).
**Row 8:** (K8, m1, k1, m1, k8) twice (38 sts).
**Row 10:** (K9, m1, k1, m1, k9) twice (42 sts).
**Row 12:** (K10, m1, k1, m1, k10) twice (46 sts).
**Rows 13 to 33:** Beg with a p row, work 21 rows in st-st.
**Row 34:** K2tog, k to last 2 sts, k2tog (44 sts).
**Row 35:** Purl.

**Row 36:** K2tog, k16, (k2tog) 4 times, k16, k2tog (38 sts).
**Row 37:** P28, turn.
**Row 38:** S1k, k 17, turn.
**Row 39:** S1p, to end.
**Row 40:** (K1, m1) 5 times, k4, k2tog, k16, k2tog, k4, (m1, k1) 5 times (46 sts).
**Row 41:** P32, turn.
**Row 42:** S1k, k17, turn.
**Row 43:** S1p, p to end.
**Row 44:** K13, k2tog, k16, k2tog, k13 (44 sts).
**Row 45:** (P2, m1) twice, p36, (m1, p2) twice (48 sts).
**Row 46:** K13, (k2tog) twice, k14, (k2tog) twice, k13 (44 sts).
**Row 47:** P13, p2tog, p14, p2tog, p13 (42 sts).

**Row 48:** K11, (k2tog) twice, k12, (k2tog) twice, k11 (38 sts).
**Row 49:** P11, p2tog, p12, p2tog, p11 (36 sts).
**Row 50:** K9, (k2tog) twice, k10, (k2tog) twice, k9 (32 sts).
**Row 51:** P9, p2tog, p10, p2tog, p9 (30 sts).
**Row 52:** K7, (k2tog) twice, k8, (k2tog) twice, k7 (26 sts).
**Row 53:** P7, p2tog, p8, p2tog, p7 (24 sts).
**Row 54:** K5, (k2tog) twice, k6, (k2tog) twice, k5 (20 sts).
**Row 55:** P5, p2tog, p6, p2tog, p5 (18 sts).
**Row 56:** K1, (k2tog) 3 times, k4, (k2tog) 3 times, k1 (12 sts).
Cast off pwise.

## Front legs (make 2)

Beg at top, using the thumb method and E, cast on 12 sts.
**Row 1 (WS):** P9, turn.
**Row 2:** S1k, k5, turn.
**Row 3:** S1p, p to end.
**Rows 4 to 11:** Work 8 rows in st-st.
**Row 12:** K3, (k2tog, k2) twice, k1 (10 sts).
**Rows 13 to 15:** Beg with a p row, work 3 rows in st-st.
Cast off.

## Toes for front legs (make 6)

Beg at toe, using the thumb method and E, cast on 10 sts, WS facing to beg.
**Rows 1 and 2:** P 1 row, then k 1 row.
**Row 3:** (P2tog) to end (5 sts).
**Rows 4 to 7:** Work 4 rows in st-st.
Cast off.

## Hind legs (make 2)

Beg at hip, using the thumb method and E, cast on 6 sts.

**Row 1 (WS):** Purl.

**Row 2:** K1, (m1, k1) to end (11 sts).

**Rows 3 to 17:** Beg with a p row, work 15 rows in st-st.

Place a marker on last row and keep the marker on RS.

**Rows 18 to 37:** Work 20 rows in st-st. Place a marker on last row and keep the marker on RS.

**Rows 38 to 55:** Work 18 rows in st-st. Cast off.

## Toes for hind legs (make 6)

Beg at toe, using the thumb method and E, cast on 10 sts, WS facing to beg.

**Rows 1 and 2:** P 1 row, then k 1 row.

**Row 3:** (P2tog) to end (5 sts).

**Rows 4 to 9:** Work 6 rows in st-st. Cast off.

## Eyes (make 2)

Beg at centre of pupil, using the thumb method and F, cast on 7 sts.

**Row 1 (RS):** Change to A and k 1 row.

**Row 2:** P1, (m1, p1) to end (13 sts).

**Row 3:** Change to E and k 1 row.

**Row 4:** K2, (m1, k3) 3 times, m1, k2 (17 sts).

**Rows 5 to 7:** Beg with a k row, work 3 rows in st-st ending with a RS row.

**Row 8:** P2tog, (p1, p2tog) to end (11 sts).

**Row 9:** K2tog, (k1, k2tog) to end (7 sts). Thread yarn through sts on needle, pull tight and secure by threading yarn a second time through sts.

## Crown

Beg at lower edge, using the thumb method and D, cast on 19 sts, WS facing to beg.

**Rows 1 to 10:** Beg with a p row, work 10 rows in st-st, ending with a RS row.

**Picot edge:** K1, (yf, k2tog) to end.

**Rows 12 to 21:** Beg with a k row, work 10 rows in st-st. Cast off pwise.

## Making up Frog

### Body and head

Gather round cast-off stitches, pull tight and secure. Sew up row ends of body and head and stuff. Bring marker and seam at lower edge together and sew across cast-on stitches.

### Front legs and toes

Gather round cast-on stitches of toes, pull tight and secure. Cut 6 lengths of chenille stick each 2in (5cm) in length and place a piece of chenille stick into gathered stitches on the wrong side of each toe with excess of chenille stick at top end. Sew up row ends of toes around chenille sticks. With right side of knitting outside, sew together row ends of cast-off stitches of front legs. Place three toes into each front leg and sew toes to cast-off stitches of front legs using mattress stitch all the way round. Sew up row ends of front legs and stuff. Sew front legs to Frog.

### Hind legs and toes

Work toes as toes for front legs. Sew up row ends of hind legs from ankle to nearest marker and stuff this part, pushing stuffing in with tweezers or tip of scissors, and sew across row with marker. Sew up row ends to next marker, stuff next section and sew across row with marker. Sew up row ends of final section, stuff final section and gather round cast-on stitches, pull tight and secure. Sew hind legs to Frog.

### Eyes and features

Sew up row ends of eyes, leaving a gap, stuff and sew up gap. Sew eyes to head around lower edge. Using picture as a guide, embroider mouth in dark green using stem stitch, and two nostrils in dark green, making a vertical chain stitch for each nostril, and then a second chain stitch on top of first chain stitch.

### Crown

Sew up row ends of crown and fold crown along picot row. Oversew lower edge and sew crown to Frog.

## How to make Prince

### Shoes, legs, body and head

Make shoes, legs, body and head as for Cinderella in Rags on page 72, using F for shoes, A for legs, G for lower body, H for upper body and B for head.

### Breeches and tunic

Make breeches and tunic as for Prince in Cinderella on page 75, using H for breeches, beg in I and change to H for tunic.

### Sleeves, hands and hair

Make sleeves and hands and hair as
for Jack's Mother on page 45 using H
for sleeves, B for hands and J for hair.

### Cuffs, collar of cloak, cloak, brooch and crown

Make cuffs, collar of cloak, cloak, brooch
and crown as for Prince in Cinderella on
pages 78–9, using I for cuffs, collar of cloak
and cloak, D for brooch and K for crown.

## Making up Prince

### Shoes, legs, body and head

Make up shoes, legs, body and head as
for Cinderella in Rags on page 73.

### Breeches and tunic

Make up breeches and tunic as for Prince
in Cinderella on page 78.

### Sleeves and hands, features and hair

Make up sleeves and hands and hair and
work features as for Jack's Mother on
pages 45–6.

### Cuffs, collar of cloak, cloak and brooch and crown

Make up cuffs, collar of cloak, cloak,
brooch and crown as for Prince in
Cinderella on page 79.

There once was a prince who was looking for a wife, but only a real princess would do. One night, during a terrible storm, there was a knock on the front door. There, bedraggled and wet, stood a princess. She promised she was a real princess, but how would he know?

# THE PRINCESS & THE PEA

# Information you'll need

## Finished sizes

Princess measures 6½in (16.5cm) high
Bed measures 10in (25cm) high
Prince measures 8½in (22 cm) high

## Materials

### Any DK (US: light worsted) yarn

**Note:** amounts are approximate
10g rose pink (A)
15g pale pink (B)
10g white (C)
10g bright pink (D)
10g brown (E)
80g pale brown (F)
5g bright green (G)
25g blue (H)
25g orange (I)
40g medium green (J)
25g yellow (K)
10g black (L)
5g grey (M)
20g dark green (N)
20g purple (O)
5g mustard (P)
5g lemon (Q)
Oddments of black, red and pale pink for embroidery
1 pair of 3.25mm (UK10:US3) needles and a spare needle of the same size
Knitters' blunt-ended pins and a needle for sewing up
Tweezers for stuffing small parts (optional)
Acrylic toy stuffing
Red pencil for shading cheeks

## Tension

26 sts x 34 rows measure 4in (10cm) square over st-st using 3.25mm needles and DK yarn before stuffing.

## Working instructions

Sew up all row-end seams on right side using mattress stitch, unless otherwise stated; a one-stitch seam allowance has been allowed for this.

# How to make Princess

### Shoes, legs, body and head
Make shoes, legs, body and head as for Princess in the Frog Prince on page 106, using A for shoes, B for legs, C for lower body, D for bodice and B for neck and head.

### Skirt of dress
Make skirt of dress as for Princess in the Frog Prince on page 106, beg in C, change to A and then cont in D.

### Sleeves and hands (make 2)
Make sleeves and hands as for Jack on page 41, using D for sleeves and B for hands.

### Neckband
Make neckband as for Princess in the Frog Prince on page 106 using D.

### Hair
Make hair as for Jack on page 42 using E.

## Making up Princess

### Shoes, legs, body and head, skirt, sleeves and hands, and neckband
Make up shoes, legs, body, head, skirt of dress, sleeves and hands and neckband as for Princess in the Frog Prince on page 106.

### Features
Work features as for Jack on page 43.

### Hair and plaits
Make up hair as for Jack on page 43. To make two plaits, take six strands of yarn to match hair 16in (40cm) long for each plait and lay them in a bundle. Tie a knot at centre of bundle then fold bundle in half. Divide into three and plait for 1½in (4cm). Tie a knot and trim ends to ⅓in (8mm). Sew plaits to sides of head.

## How to make Bed

### Base of bed
Using the thumb method and F, cast on 26 sts, RS facing to beg.
**Rows 1 to 60:** Beg with a k row, work 60 rows in st-st.
**Rows 61 and 62:** Work 2 rows in g-st.
**Rows 63 to 72:** Beg with a k row, work 10 rows in st-st.
**Rows 73 and 74:** Work 2 rows in g-st.
**Rows 75 and 76:** Cont in st-st and cast on 10 sts at beg of next 2 rows (46 sts).
**Rows 77 to 134:** Work 58 rows in st-st.
**Row 135:** Cast off 10 sts at beg of row (36 sts).
**Row 136:** Cast off 10 sts at beg of row and k to end (26 sts).
**Rows 137 to 148:** Beg with a k row, work 12 rows in st-st.
Cast off kwise.

## Pea

Using the thumb method and G, cast on 12 sts, WS facing to beg.

**Rows 1 to 3:** Beg with a p row, work 3 rows in st-st.

Cast off.

## Bed head and foot
## (make 2 pieces)

**Note:** Foll individual instructions for bed head and bed foot.

Beg at lower edge, using the thumb method and F, cast on 30 sts.

**Row 1 (WS):** Purl.

**Rows 2 and 3:** Work 2 rows in g-st.

**Rows 4 to 15:** Beg with a k row, work 12 rows in st-st.

**Rows 16 and 17:** Work 2 rows in g-st.

**For bed head**

**Rows 18 to 57:** Beg with a k row, work 40 rows in st-st.

Cast off.

**For bed foot**

**Rows 18 to 47:** Beg with a k row, work 30 rows in st-st.

Cast off.

## Twenty mattresses

Using the thumb method and H, cast on 24 sts, WS facing to beg.

**Rows 1 to 59:** Beg with a p row, work 59 rows in st-st.

**Row 60:** Using the knitting-on method, cast on 65 sts at beg of row and p this row (89 sts).

**Row 61:** Cast on 41 sts at beg of row and k this row (130 sts).

**Row 62:** Purl.

**Row 63:** Knit.

**Row 64:** Change to I and k 1 row.

**Rows 65 to 67:** Beg with a k row, work 3 rows in rev st-st.

**Row 68:** Change to J and k 1 row.

**Rows 69 to 71:** Beg with a k row, work 3 rows in rev st-st.

**Row 72:** Change to K and k 1 row.

**Rows 73 to 77:** Beg with a k row, work 5 rows in rev st-st.

**Row 78:** Change to H and k 1 row.

**Rows 79 to 81:** Beg with a k row, work 3 rows in rev st-st.

**Row 82:** Change to I and k 1 row.

**Rows 83 to 85:** Beg with a k row, work 3 rows in rev st-st.

**Row 86:** Change to J and k 1 row.

**Rows 87 to 89:** Beg with a k row, work 3 rows in rev st-st.

**Row 90:** Change to K and k 1 row.
**Rows 91 to 93:** Beg with a k row, work 3 rows in rev st-st.
**Row 94:** Change to H and k 1 row.
**Rows 95 to 99:** Beg with a k row, work 5 rows in rev st-st.
**Row 100:** Change to I and k 1 row.
**Rows 101 to 103:** Beg with a k row, work 3 rows in rev st-st.
**Row 104:** Change to J and k 1 row.
**Rows 105 to 107:** Beg with a k row, work 3 rows in rev st-st.
**Row 108:** Change to K and k 1 row.
**Rows 109 to 111:** Beg with a k row, work 3 rows in rev st-st.
**Row 112:** Change to H and k 1 row.
**Rows 113 to 115:** Beg with a k row, work 3 rows in rev st-st.
**Row 116:** Change to I and k 1 row.
**Rows 117 to 121:** Beg with a k row, work 5 rows in rev st-st.
**Row 122:** Change to J and k 1 row.
**Rows 123 to 125:** Beg with a k row, work 3 rows in rev st-st.

**Row 126:** Change to K and k 1 row.
**Rows 127 to 129:** Beg with a k row, work 3 rows in rev st-st.
**Row 130:** Change to H and k 1 row.
**Rows 131 to 133:** Beg with a k row, work 3 rows in rev st-st.
**Row 134:** Change to I and k 1 row.
**Rows 135 to 137:** Beg with a k row, work 3 rows in rev st-st.
**Row 138:** Change to J and k 1 row.
**Rows 139 to 143:** Beg with a k row, work 5 rows in rev st-st.
**Row 144:** Change to K and k 1 row.
**Rows 145 to 147:** Beg with a k row, work 3 rows in rev st-st.
**Row 148:** Cast off 65 sts kwise at beg of row, k23 (24 sts now on RH needle), cast off rem 41 sts and fasten off (24 sts).
**Rows 149 to 207:** Rejoin yarn to rem sts and beg with a p row, work 59 rows in st-st.
Cast off.

### Pillow
Using the thumb method and J, cast on 20 sts, WS facing to beg.
**Rows 1 to 35:** Beg with a p row, work 35 rows in st-st.
Cast off.

### Eiderdown
### (make 2 pieces)
Using the thumb method and J, cast on 40 sts, WS facing to beg.
**Row 1:** Purl.
**Rows 2 and 3:** Join in C and working in stripes, carrying yarn loosely up side of work, work 2 rows in st-st.
**Rows 4 and 5:** Using J, work 2 rows in st-st.
**Rows 6 to 53:** Rep rows 2 to 5, 12 times more.
Cast off in J.

## Making up Bed

### Base of bed and pea
Sew up corners of base and stuff. With right side of stocking stitch outside, roll pea up from row ends to row ends, gather round top and bottom, pull tight and secure. Sew pea to top of Bed. Sew up top of base all the way round to complete.

### Bed head and foot
Oversew cast-on and cast-off stitches of bed head and foot and lightly stuff, keeping work flat. Sew up row ends at sides. Sew bed head and foot to ends of base of Bed, sewing garter stitch rows of head and foot to garter stitch rows of base of Bed.

### Twenty mattresses
Sew up striped row ends of mattresses and sew up base. Stuff mattresses and sew up top.

### Pillow
Sew up cast-on and cast-off stitches of pillow and sew up row ends at one end. Stuff pillow and sew up remaining row ends.

### Eiderdown
Place wrong sides of two pieces of eiderdown together and using mattress stitch, sew around outside edge.

# How to make Prince

### Shoes, legs, body and head

Make shoes, legs, body and head as for Cinderella in Rags on page 72, using L for shoes, C for legs, M for lower body, N for upper body and B for head.

### Breeches and tunic

Make breeches and tunic as for Prince in Cinderella on page 78, using N for breeches, beg in O and change to N for tunic.

### Sleeves, hands and hair

Make sleeves, hands and hair as for Jack's Mother on page 45, using N for sleeves, B for hands and E for hair.

### Cuffs, collar of cloak, cloak, brooch and crown

Make cuffs, collar of cloak, cloak, brooch and crown as for Prince in Cinderella on pages 78–9, using O for cuffs, collar of cloak and cloak, P for brooch and Q for crown.

# Making up Prince

### Shoes, legs, body and head

Make up shoes, legs, body and head as for Cinderella in Rags on page 73.

### Breeches and tunic

Make up breeches and tunic as for Prince in Cinderella on page 78.

### Sleeves and hands, features and hair

Make up sleeves, hands and hair and work features as for Jack's Mother on pages 45–6.

### Cuffs, collar of cloak, cloak, brooch and crown

Make up cuffs, collar of cloak, cloak, brooch and crown as for Prince in Cinderella on page 79.

There was once a little girl who lived near the dark woods. Everybody called her Little Red Riding Hood. One day her mother asked her to take a basket of food to her grandma who lived in the woods and told her not to speak to anyone on the way...

# LITTLE RED RIDING HOOD

# Information you'll need

### Finished size
Red Riding Hood measures 7in (18cm) high
Grandma measures 9in (23cm) high
Bed measures 10in (25cm) long
Wolf measures 6¼in (16cm) high
Wood Cutter measures 9in (23cm) high

### Materials
**Any DK (US: light worsted) yarn**
**Note:** amounts are approximate
5g cerise (A)
15g pale pink (B)
40g white (C)
15g red (D)
5g lemon (E)
5g brown (F)
100g pale brown (G)
5g gold (H)
10g lilac (I)
5g pale green (J)
15g silver grey (K)
20g golden cream (L)
15g beige (M)
20g dark grey (N)
5g black (O)
10g mustard (P)
10g dark brown (Q)
10g dark green (R)
Oddments of black, red, pale pink, green
and white for embroidery

1 pair of 3.25mm (UK10:US3) needles and
a spare needle of the same size
Knitters' blunt-ended pins and a needle for
sewing up
Tweezers for stuffing small parts (optional)
Acrylic toy stuffing
Red pencil for shading cheeks
1 drinking straw

### Tension
26 sts x 34 rows measure 4in (10cm)
square over st-st using 3.25mm needles
and DK yarn before stuffing.

### Working instructions
Sew up all row-end seams on right side
using mattress stitch, unless otherwise
stated; a one-stitch seam allowance has
been allowed for this.

# How to make Little Red Riding Hood

## Shoes, legs, body and head

### Right leg

Beg at sole of shoe, using the thumb method and A, cast on 10 sts.

Place a marker on cast-on edge between the 4th and 5th st of the sts just cast on.

**Row 1 (WS):** Purl.

**Row 2:** K1, (m1, k1) to end (19 sts).

**Rows 3 to 5:** Beg with a p row, work 3 rows in st-st.

### Shape shoe

**Row 6:** K1, (k2tog) 7 times, k4 (12 sts).

**Rows 7 to 23:** Change to B for leg and beg with a p row, work 17 rows in st-st. Break yarn and set aside.

### Left leg

Beg at sole of shoe, using the thumb method and A, cast on 10 sts.

Place a marker on cast-on edge between the 6th and 7th st of the sts just cast on.

**Row 1 (WS):** Purl.

**Row 2:** K1, (m1, k1) to end (19 sts).

**Rows 3 to 5:** Beg with a p row, work 3 rows in st-st.

### Shape shoe

**Row 6:** K4, (k2tog) 7 times, k1 (12 sts).

**Rows 7 to 23:** Change to B for leg and beg with a p row, work 17 rows in st-st.

### Join legs

**Row 24:** Change to C for lower body and k across sts of left leg, and then with the same yarn cont k across sts of right leg (24 sts).

**Rows 25 to 29:** Beg with a p row, work 5 rows in st-st.

**Rows 30 to 41:** Change to D for upper body and work 12 rows in st-st.

**Rows 42 and 43:** Change to B for head and work 2 rows in st-st.

**Row 44:** K3, (m1, k6), 3 times, m1, k3 (28 sts).

**Rows 45 to 51:** Beg with a p row, work 7 rows in st-st.

### Shape top of head

**Row 52:** (K2tog, k2) to end (21 sts).

**Row 53 and foll alt row:** Purl.

**Row 54:** (K2tog, k1) to end (14 sts).

**Row 56:** (K2tog) to end (7 sts).

Thread yarn through sts on needle and leave loose.

## Skirt

Beg at lower edge, using the thumb method and E, cast on 50 sts and beg in g-st, RS facing to beg.

**Rows 1 to 4:** Work 4 rows in g-st.

**Rows 5 to 16:** Change to D and beg with a k row, work 12 rows in st-st.

**Row 17:** (K2tog, k3) to end (40 sts).

**Rows 18 to 20:** Beg with a p row, work 3 rows in st-st.

**Row 21:** (K2tog, k2) to end (30 sts).

Cast off pwise.

## Sleeves and hands (make 2)

Beg at shoulder, using the thumb method and D, cast on 4 sts.

**Row 1 (WS):** Purl.

**Row 2:** K1, m1, k to last st, m1, k1 (6 sts).

**Rows 3 to 8:** Rep rows 1 and 2, 3 times more (12 sts).

Place a marker on first and last st of the last row.

**Rows 9 to 15:** Beg with a p row, work 7 rows in st-st.

**Row 16:** K1, k2tog, (k2, k2tog) twice, k1 (9 sts).

**Rows 17 to 21:** Change to B for hand and beg with a p row, work 5 rows in st-st. Thread yarn through sts on needle, pull tight and secure by threading yarn a second time through sts.

## Cuffs (make 2)

Make cuffs as for Jack on page 42, using D.

## Hair

Make hair as for Jack on page 42, using F.

## Hood and cape

### Cape

Using the thumb method and D, cast on 46 sts and work in g-st, RS facing to beg.

**Rows 1 to 4:** Work 4 rows in g-st.

**Row 5:** Knit.

**Row 6:** K2, p to last 2 sts, k2.

**Rows 7 to 10:** Rep rows 5 and 6 twice more.

**Row 11:** *K3, (k2tog, k1) 6 times, k2; rep from * once (34 sts).

**Row 12:** As row 6.

**Row 13:** *K3, (k2tog, k1) 4 times, k2; rep from * once (26 sts).

**Row 14:** As row 6.

**Row 15:** K4, (k2tog, k2) 5 times, k2 (21 sts). Cast off in patt as set.

*little red riding hood*

### Hood

Using the thumb method and D, cast on 12 sts.

**Row 1 (WS):** K2, p end.

**Row 2:** K4, (m1, k4) twice (14 sts).

**Row 3:** K2, p to end.

**Row 4:** Knit.

**Rows 5 to 47:** Rep rows 3 and 4, 21 times and then row 3 once.

**Row 48:** K3, k2tog, k4, k2tog, k3 (12 sts). Cast off in patt as set.

## Basket and flowers

**Note:** use a double length of yarn for rim of basket and handle, treated as one strand.

### Basket

Using yarn double, the thumb method and G, cast on 20 sts and work in g-st, RS facing to beg.

**Rows 1 to 8:** Cont with a single strand of yarn and work 8 rows in g-st.

**Row 9:** (K2tog) twice, k2, (k2tog) 4 times, k2, (k2tog) twice (12 sts). Cast off in g-st.

### Handle

Using yarn double, the thumb method and G, cast on 12 sts.

Cast off pwise, using yarn double.

### Flowers (make 2 in each of D, E and H)

Using the thumb method and D, E or H, cast on 8 sts.

Thread yarn through sts on needle, pull tight and secure by threading yarn a second time through sts.

## Making up Little Red Riding Hood

### Shoes, legs, body and head
Make up shoes, legs, body and head as for Courtier in Cinderella on page 81.

### Skirt
Sew up row ends of skirt and place on doll. Sew cast-off stitches of skirt to first row of upper body all the way round.

### Sleeves, hands and cuffs
Make up sleeves, hands and cuffs as for Jack on page 43.

### Features and hair
Work features and make up hair as for Jack on page 43.

### Hood and cape
Place cape around shoulders and join beneath chin. Sew cape to neck all the way round. Fold row ends of hood in half and sew up back seam. Sew hood to top edge of cape all the way round. Make a twisted cord out of 1 strand of red, beginning with the yarn 36in (90cm) long, make a tiny bow, sew to beneath chin and knot and trim ends to 1in (2.5cm).

### Basket and flowers
Oversew row ends of basket and fold cast-off stitches in half and oversew. Sew handle to sides of basket and handle to hand. Make stems for flowers in green: cut six stems each 8in (20cm) long, thread each stem through a flower at back and fold stem in half. Place stems in a bundle, tie securely and cut ends of stems to 1in (2.5cm). Sew stems to hand.

## How to make Grandma

### Body and head
Beg at lower body, using the thumb method and C, cast on 28 sts, WS facing to beg.
Place a marker on cast-on edge at centre of the cast-on sts.
**Rows 1 to 7:** Beg with a p row, work 7 rows in st-st.
**Rows 8 to 21:** Change to I for upper body and work 14 rows in st-st.
**Rows 22 and 23:** Change to B for head and work 2 rows in st-st.

**Row 24:** *K4, (m1, k2) 4 times, k2; rep from * once (36 sts).
**Rows 25 to 39:** Beg with a p row, work 15 rows in st-st.
**Shape top of head**
**Row 40:** (K2tog, k2) to end (27 sts).
**Row 41 and foll alt row:** Purl.
**Row 42:** (K2tog, k1) to end (18 sts).
**Row 44:** (K2tog) to end (9 sts).
Thread yarn through sts on needle, pull tight and secure by threading yarn a second time through sts.

## Slippers and legs (make 2)

Beg at sole of slipper, using the thumb method and J, cast on 14 sts.

**Row 1 (WS):** Purl.

**Row 2:** K2, (m1, k2) to end (20 sts).

**Rows 3 to 5:** Beg with a p row, work 3 rows in st-st.

**Rows 6 and 7:** Change to B for leg and work 2 rows in st-st.

**Shape foot**

**Row 8:** K4, (k2tog, k1) twice, (k1, k2tog) twice, k4 (16 sts).

**Row 9:** Purl.

**Row 10:** K5, (k2tog, k2) twice, k3 (14 sts).

**Rows 11 to 31:** Beg with a p row, work 21 rows in st-st.

Cast off.

## Skirt of nightdress

Beg at lower edge, using the thumb method and I, cast on 60 sts and beg in g-st, RS facing to beg.

**Rows 1 to 8:** Work 8 rows in g-st.

**Rows 9 to 24:** Change to C and beg with a k row work 16 rows in st-st.

**Row 25:** (K2tog, k3) to end (48 sts).

**Rows 26 to 28:** Beg with a p row, work 3 rows in st-st.

**Row 29:** (K2tog, k2) to end (36 sts).

Cast off kwise.

## Sleeves and hands (make 2)

Make sleeves and hands as for Jack's Mother on page 45, using C for sleeve and B for hand.

## Cuffs (make 2)

Make cuffs as for Jack's Mother on page 45, using C.

## Hair

Make hair as for Jack's Mother on page 45, using K.

## Mob cap

**Crown piece**

Using the thumb method and C, cast on 36 sts.

**Row 1 (WS):** Purl.

**Row 2:** K1, (m1, k2) to last st, m1, k1 (54 sts).

**Rows 3 to 9:** Beg with a p row, work 7 rows in st-st.

**Row 10:** (K2tog, k4) to end (45 sts).

**Row 11 and foll 3 alt rows:** Purl.

**Row 12:** (K2tog, k3) to end (36 sts).

**Row 14:** (K2tog, k2) to end (27 sts).

**Row 16:** (K2tog, k1) to end (18 sts).

**Row 18:** (K2tog) to end (9 sts).

Thread yarn through sts on needle, pull tight and secure by threading yarn a second time through sts.

**Cap frill**

Using the thumb method and C, cast on 100 sts and work in g-st, RS facing to beg.

**Rows 1 and 2:** Work 2 rows in g-st.

**Row 3:** (K2tog) to end (50 sts).

**Row 4:** (K2tog, k3) to end (40 sts).

Cast off in g-st.

## Shawl

Using the thumb method and I, cast on 49 sts.

**Row 1 (WS):** K1, (yf, k2tog) to last 2 sts, yf, k2tog tbl.

**Row 2:** K3tog, (yf, k2tog) to last 2 sts, yf, k2tog tbl (47 sts).

**Rows 3 to 23:** Rep row 2, 21 times more (5 sts).

**Row 24:** K3tog, yf, k2tog tbl (3 sts).

**Row 25:** K3tog tbl.

Fasten off.

# Making up Grandma

### Body and head

Sew up row ends of head and body and stuff. With seam at centre back, bring seam and marker together and sew up cast-on stitches. To shape neck, take a double length of yarn to match upper body and sew a running stitch round last row of upper body, sewing in and out of every half stitch. Pull tight, knot yarn and sew ends into neck.

### Slippers and legs

Fold cast-on stitches of slippers in half and oversew. Sew up row ends of slippers and place a ball of stuffing into toes. Sew up row ends of legs and stuff legs. With seam of each leg at centre back, sew across cast-off stitches. With toes pointing forwards, sew cast-off stitches of legs to cast-on stitches of body at lower edge.

### Skirt of nightdress

Sew up row ends of skirt of nightdress and place on doll. Sew cast-off stitches at waist to first row of upper body all the way round.

### Sleeves, hands and cuffs

Make up sleeves, hands and cuffs as for Jack's Mother on page 45.

### Features and hair

Embroider features and make up hair as for Jack's Mother on page 46.

### Mob cap

Sew up row ends of crown piece of mob cap and stuff top lightly. Sew lower edge of crown piece to head all the way round. Place cap frill around head, sew up row ends and sew cast-off stitches of frill to cast-on stitches of crown piece.

### Shawl

Place shawl around shoulders of doll and sew in place.

# How to make Bed

### Base and mattress

Using the thumb method and C, cast on 30 sts, RS facing to beg.
**Rows 1 to 70:** Beg with a k row, work 70 rows in st-st.
**Rows 71 and 72:** Work 2 rows in g-st.
**Rows 73 to 86:** Change to G and beg with a k row, work 14 rows in st-st.
**Rows 87 and 88:** Work 2 rows in g-st.
**Rows 89 and 90:** Cont in st-st and cast on 12 sts at beg of next 2 rows (54 sts).
**Rows 91 to 158:** Beg with a k row, work 68 rows in st-st.
**Row 159:** Cast off 12 sts kwise at beg of row (42 sts).
**Row 160:** Cast off 12 sts pwise at beg of row and k to end (30 sts).
**Rows 161 to 174:** Beg with a k row, work 14 rows in st-st.
Cast off kwise.

### Bed head and foot (make 2 pieces)

**Note:** Foll individual instructions for bed head and bed foot.
Beg at lower edge, using the thumb method and G, cast on 34 sts.
**Row 1 (WS):** Purl.
**Rows 2 and 3:** Work 2 rows in g-st.
**Rows 4 to 17:** Beg with a k row, work 14 rows in st-st.
**Rows 18 and 19:** Work 2 rows in g-st.
**For bed head**
**Rows 20 to 69:** Beg with a k row, work 50 rows in st-st.
Cast off.
**For bed foot**
**Rows 20 to 49:** Beg with a k row, work 30 rows in st-st.
Cast off.

## Pillow

Using the thumb method and L, cast on 30 sts and work in g-st, RS facing to beg.
**Rows 1 to 45:** Work 45 rows in g-st.
Cast off in g-st.

## Eiderdown

Using the thumb method and L, cast on 45 sts and work in g-st, RS facing to beg.
**Rows 1 to 4:** Work 4 rows in g-st.
Join in M and work L and M in stripes, carrying yarn loosely up side of work.
**Rows 5 to 10:** Using M, work 6 rows in g-st.
**Rows 11 to 16:** Using L, work 6 rows in g-st.
**Rows 17 to 70:** Rep rows 5 to 16, 4 times more and then rows 5 to 10 once.
**Rows 71 to 75:** Using L, work 5 rows in g-st.
Cast off in g-st.

### Edging

Work edging along row ends. With RS facing and using L, pick up and knit 39 sts along edge.
**Rows 1 to 4:** Work 4 rows in g-st.
Cast off in g-st.
Rep for opposite edge.

## Making up Bed

### Base and mattress

Sew up corners of base and stuff. Sew mattress to base all the way round.

### Head and foot

Oversew cast-on and cast-off stitches of bed head and bed foot and stuff lightly, keeping work flat. Using mattress stitch, sew up row ends at sides. Sew bed head and foot to ends of Bed, sewing garter stitch rows of head and foot to garter stitch rows of Bed.

### Pillow

Sew up cast-on and cast-off stitches of pillow and sew up row ends at one end. Stuff pillow and sew up remaining row ends.

### Eiderdown

Weave in ends.

## How to make Wolf

Make Wolf as Wolf in Three Little Pigs on page 101, using N for base of body and joining in K for belly, N for head, hind legs, forearms and ears, and beg in N and changing to K for tail. Using picture as a guide, embroider teeth in white.

# How to make Wood Cutter and Axe

### Shoes, legs, body and head
Make shoes, legs, body and head as for Cinderella in Rags on page 72, using O for shoes, B for legs, C for lower body, P for upper body and B for head.

### Trousers
#### First leg
Beg at lower edge, using the thumb method and Q, cast on 22 sts, RS facing to beg.
**Rows 1 and 2:** P 1 row then k 1 row.
**Rows 3 to 20:** Beg with a k row, work 18 rows in st-st.
**Rows 21 and 22:** Cast off 2 sts at beg of next 2 rows (18 sts).
Break yarn and set aside.
#### Second leg
Work as first leg but do not break yarn.

#### Join legs
**Row 23:** With RS facing, k across sts of second leg, and then with the same yarn cont k across sts of first leg (36 sts).
**Rows 24 to 30:** Beg with a p row, work 7 rows in st-st.
Cast off.

### Belt
Using the thumb method and O, cast on 36 sts and work in g-st, RS facing to beg.
**Rows 1 to 3:** Work 3 rows in g-st.
Cast off in g-st.

### Sleeves, hands and cuffs
Make sleeves, hands and cuffs as for Jack's Mother on page 45, using P for sleeves, B for hands and P for cuffs.

### Hair
Make hair as for Jack's Mother on page 45, using G.

### Waistcoat
Beg at lower edge, using the thumb method and R, cast on 36 sts and work in g-st, RS facing to beg.
**Rows 1 to 13:** Work 13 rows in g-st, ending with a RS row.
#### Divide for fronts and back
**Row 14:** K5, cast off next 4 sts (6 sts now on RH needle), k17, cast off next 4 sts, k4 (28 sts).
**Row 15:** K5, turn and work on these 5 sts.
**Rows 16 to 31:** Work 16 rows in g-st, ending with a RS row.
Cast off in g-st and fasten off.
Rejoin yarn to rem sts.
**Row 32:** K18, turn and work on these 18 sts.
**Rows 33 to 48:** Work 16 rows in g-st, ending with a RS row.
Cast off in g-st and fasten off.
**Rows 49 to 65:** Rejoin yarn to rem 5 sts and work 17 rows in g-st, ending with a RS row.
Cast off in g-st.

# Making up Wood Cutter and Axe

## Hat

Beg at brim, using the thumb method
and N, cast on 54 sts and beg in g-st,
RS facing to beg.

**Rows 1 and 2:** Work 2 rows in g-st.
**Row 3:** (K2tog, k4) to end (45 sts).
**Row 4:** Knit.
**Row 5:** (K2tog, k3) to end (36 sts).
**Rows 6 to 12:** Beg with a p row, work
7 rows in st-st.
**Row 13:** (K2tog, k2) to end (27 sts).
**Row 14 and foll alt row:** Purl.
**Row 15:** (K2tog, k1) to end (18 sts).
**Row 17:** (K2tog) to end (9 sts).
Thread yarn through sts on needle,
pull tight and secure by threading yarn
a second time through sts.

## Axe

Make Axe as for Axe in Jack and the
Beanstalk on page 59, using M for
handle and K for head of Axe.

## Shoes, legs, body and head

Make up shoes, legs, body and head as
for Cinderella in Rags on page 73.

## Trousers

Sew up row ends of legs of trousers from
lower edge to crotch. Sew round crotch
and sew up row ends at centre back.
Place trousers on doll and sew cast-off
stitches at waist to first row of upper
body all the way round.

## Belt

Place belt around waist, oversew row
ends and sew lower and upper edge
of belt to doll all the way round.

## Sleeves, hands and cuffs

Make up sleeves, hands and cuffs as for
Jack's Mother on page 45.

## Features and hair

Work features and make up hair as for
Jack's Mother on page 46.

## Waistcoat

Sew up shoulder seams of waistcoat and
place on doll. Sew back of waistcoat to
neck at back.

## Hat

Sew up row ends of hat and oversew brim.
Lightly stuff top of hat, place hat on head
and pin and sew hat to head using back
stitch on right side of base of brim, sewing
through hat to head.

## Axe

Make up Axe as for Axe in Jack and the
Beanstalk on page 59.

Once upon a time there was a little girl called Goldilocks who lived at the edge of a forest. One day she wandered into the forest and lost her way. She was very frightened until she saw a sweet cottage in the distance. The cottage belonged to three bears...

# GOLDILOCKS & THE THREE BEARS

# Information you'll need

### Finished sizes

Goldilocks measures 6½in (16.5cm) high
Three Bears measure 5½in (14cm) to
11½in (29cm) high
Bowls of porridge and spoons measure
1½in (4cm) to 3in (8cm) across

### Materials

**Any DK (US: light worsted) yarn**
**Note:** amounts are approximate
5g medium blue (A)
10g pale pink (B)
10g white (C)
10g mauve (D)
5g dark purple (E)
10g gold (F)
125g brown (G)
10g dark grey (H)
15g royal blue (I)
15g bright pink (J)
10g red (K)
5g aqua blue (L)
5g buttermilk (M)
10g silver grey (N)
Oddments of black, red and pale pink
for embroidery

1 pair of 3.25mm (UK10:US3) needles and
a spare needle of the same size
Knitters' blunt-ended pins and a needle for
sewing up
Tweezers for stuffing small parts (optional)
Acrylic toy stuffing
Red pencil for shading cheeks
3 chenille sticks

### Tension

26 sts x 34 rows measure 4in (10cm)
square over st-st using 3.25mm needles
and DK yarn before stuffing.

### Working instructions

Sew up all row-end seams on right side
using mattress stitch, unless otherwise
stated; a one-stitch seam allowance has
been allowed for this.

# How to make Goldilocks

### Shoes, legs, body and head
Make shoes, legs, body and head as for Courtier in Cinderella on page 80, using A for shoes, B for legs, C for lower body, D for upper body.

### Skirt and sash
Make skirt as skirt of dress for Princess in the Frog Prince on page 106, beg in C for skirt, changing to E and then cont in D. Make sash as for Princess in the Frog Prince on page 106, using E.

### Sleeves and hands
Make sleeves and hands as for Jack on page 41, using D for sleeves.

### Cuffs and collar
Make cuffs and collar as for Courtier in Cinderella on page 81, using C.

### Hair
Make hair as for Jack on page 42, using F.

### Bows (make 2)
Using the thumb method and A, cast on 15 sts, RS facing to beg.
Cast off pwise.

# Making up Goldilocks

### Shoes, legs, body and head
Make up shoes, legs, body and head as for Courtier in Cinderella on page 81.

### Skirt and sash
Make up skirt and sash as for Princess in the Frog Prince on page 107.

### Sleeves and hands
Make up sleeves and hands as for Jack on page 43.

### Cuffs and collar
Make up cuffs and collar as for Courtier on page 81.

### Features and hair
Work features and make up hair as for Jack on page 43.

### Golden locks and bows
Using F, make two bundles of 20 strands of yarn, each measuring 12in (30cm), tie these bundles in the middle and fold in half. If yarn used is suitable, unravel all strands for a 'frizzy' look. Sew bunches to head, one at each side, and trim ends to waist. For bows, oversew row ends to make a ring then wind matching yarn round centre to create a bow shape and secure and sew bows to top of bunches.

# How to make Bears

### Bodies

**Body for Father Bear (make 2 pieces)**

**First leg**

Beg at lower edge, using the thumb method and G, cast on 10 sts.

**Row 1 (WS):** Purl.

**Row 2:** K1, (m1, k2) 4 times, m1, k1 (15 sts).

**Rows 3 to 21:** Beg with a p row, work 19 rows in st-st.

Break yarn and set aside.

**Second leg**

Work as first leg but do not break yarn.

**Join legs**

**Row 22:** With RS facing, k across sts of second leg, turn and using the knitting-on method, cast on 5 sts, turn and with the same yarn cont k across sts of second leg (35 sts).

**Rows 23 to 57:** Beg with a p row, work 35 rows in st-st.

**Row 58:** (K2tog, k5) to end (30 sts).

**Rows 59 to 61:** Beg with a p row, work 3 rows in st-st.

**Row 62:** (K2tog, k4) to end (25 sts).

**Row 63:** Purl.

**Row 64:** (K2tog, k3) to end (20 sts).

Cast off pwise.

**Body for Mother Bear (make 2 pieces)**

**First leg**

Beg at lower edge, using the thumb method and G, cast on 8 sts.

**Row 1 (WS):** Purl.

**Row 2:** K1, (m1, k2) 3 times, m1, k1 (12 sts).

**Rows 3 to 17:** Beg with a p row, work 15 rows in st-st.

Break yarn and set aside.

**Second leg**

Work as first leg but do not break yarn.

**Join legs**

**Row 18:** With RS facing, k across sts of second leg, turn and using the knitting-on method, cast on 4 sts, turn and with the same yarn cont k across sts of second leg (28 sts).

**Rows 19 to 43:** Beg with a p row, work 25 rows in st-st.

**Row 44:** (K2tog, k5) to end (24 sts).

**Rows 45 to 47:** Beg with a p row, work 3 rows in st-st.

**Row 48:** (K2tog, k4) to end (20 sts).

**Row 49:** Purl.

**Row 50:** (K2tog, k3) to end (16 sts). Cast off pwise.

**Body for Baby Bear (make 2 pieces)**

**First leg**

Beg at lower edge, using the thumb method and G, cast on 6 sts.

**Row 1 (WS):** Purl.

**Row 2:** K1, (m1, k2) twice, m1, k1 (9 sts).

**Rows 3 to 11:** Beg with a p row, work 9 rows in st-st.

Break yarn and set aside.

**Second leg**

Work as first leg but do not break yarn.

**Join legs**

**Row 12:** With RS facing, k across sts of second leg, turn and using the knitting-on method, cast on 2 sts, turn and with the same yarn cont k across sts of second leg (20 sts).

**Rows 13 to 27:** Beg with a p row, work 15 rows in st-st.

**Row 28:** (K2tog, k3) to end (16 sts).

**Row 29:** Purl.

**Row 30:** (K2tog, k2) to end (12 sts). Cast off pwise.

## Head

**Head for Father Bear**

Beg at lower edge, using the thumb method and G, cast on 38 sts.

**Row 1 (WS):** Purl.

**Row 2:** K2, (m1, k2) to end (56 sts).

**Rows 3 to 7:** Beg with a p row, work 5 rows in st-st.

**Row 8:** K27, m1, k2, m1, k27 (58 sts).

**Row 9 and foll 5 alt rows:** Purl.

**Row 10:** K28, m1, k2, m1, k28 (60 sts).

**Row 12:** K29, m1, k2, m1, k29 (62 sts).

**Row 14:** K30, m1, k2, m1, k30 (64 sts).

**Row 16:** K31, m1, k2, m1, k31 (66 sts).

**Row 18:** K32, m1, k2, m1, k32 (68 sts).

**Row 20:** K33, m1, k2, m1, k33 (70 sts).

**Rows 21 to 25:** Beg with a p row, work
5 rows in st-st.

**Shape nose**

**Row 26:** K28, cast off 14 sts (29 sts now
on RH needle), k to end (56 sts).

**Rows 27 to 29:** Push rem sts tog and beg
with a p row, work 3 rows in st-st.

**Row 30:** (K2tog, k5) to end (48 sts).

**Row 31 and foll 4 alt rows:** Purl.

**Row 32:** (K2tog, k4) to end (40 sts).

**Row 34:** (K2tog, k3) to end (32 sts).

**Row 36:** (K2tog, k2) to end (24 sts).

**Row 38:** (K2tog, k1) to end (16 sts).

**Row 40:** (K2tog) to end (8 sts).

Thread yarn through sts on needle,
pull tight and secure by threading yarn
a second time through sts.

## Head for Mother Bear

Beg at lower edge, using the thumb
method and G, cast on 30 sts.

**Row 1 (WS):** Purl.

**Row 2:** K2, (m1, k2) to end (44 sts).

**Rows 3 to 7:** Beg with a p row, work
5 rows in st-st.

**Row 8:** K21, m1, k2, m1, k21 (46 sts).

**Row 9 and foll 2 alt rows:** Purl.

**Row 10:** K22, m1, k2, m1, k22 (48 sts).

**Row 12:** K23, m1, k2, m1, k23 (50 sts).

**Row 14:** K24, m1, k2, m1, k24 (52 sts).

**Rows 15 to 19:** Beg with a p row, work 5
rows in st-st.

**Shape nose**

**Row 20:** K20, cast off 12 sts (21 sts
now on RH needle), k to end (40 sts).

**Rows 21 to 23:** Push rem sts tog and beg
with a p row, work 3 rows in st-st.

**Row 24:** (K2tog, k3) to end (32 sts).

**Row 25 and foll 2 alt rows:** Purl.

**Row 26:** (K2tog, k2) to end (24 sts).

**Row 28:** (K2tog, k1) to end (16 sts).

**Row 30:** (K2tog) to end (8 sts).

Thread yarn through sts on needle,
pull tight and secure by threading yarn
a second time through sts.

## Head for Baby Bear

Beg at lower edge, using the thumb
method and G, cast on 22 sts.

**Row 1 (WS):** Purl.

**Row 2:** K2, (m1, k2) to end (32 sts).

**Rows 3 to 5:** Beg with a p row, work
3 rows in st-st.

**Row 6:** K15, m1, k2, m1, k15 (34 sts).

**Row 7 and foll alt row:** Purl.

**Row 8:** K16, m1, k2, m1, k16 (36 sts).

**Row 10:** K17, m1, k2, m1, k17 (38 sts).

**Rows 11 to 13:** Beg with a p row, work
3 rows in st-st.

**Shape nose**

**Row 14:** K16, cast off 6 sts (17 sts now
on RH needle), k to end (32 sts).

**Row 15 to 17:** Push rem sts tog and beg
with a p row, work 3 rows in st-st.

**Row 18:** (K2tog, k2) to end (24 sts).

**Row 19 and foll alt row:** Purl.

**Row 20:** (K2tog, k1) to end (16 sts).

**Row 22:** (K2tog) to end (8 sts).

Thread yarn through sts on needle,
pull tight and secure by threading yarn
a second time through sts.

## Arms

### Arms for Father Bear (make 2)

Beg at shoulder, using the thumb method
and G, cast on 6 sts.

**Row 1 (WS):** Purl.

**Row 2:** K1, m1, k to last st, m1, k1 (8 sts).

**Rows 3 to 22:** Rep rows 1 and 2, 10 times
more (28 sts).

**Rows 23 to 37:** Beg with a p row, work
15 rows in st-st.

**Row 38:** (K2tog) to end (14 sts).

**Row 39:** Purl.

**Row 40:** (K2tog) to end (7 sts).

Thread yarn through sts on needle,
pull tight and secure by threading yarn
a second time through sts.

### Arms for Mother Bear (make 2)

Beg at shoulder, using the thumb method
and G, cast on 6 sts.

**Row 1 (WS):** Purl.

**Row 2:** K1, m1, k to last st, m1, k1 (8 sts).

**Rows 3 to 14:** Rep rows 1 and 2, 6 times
more (20 sts).

**Rows 15 to 25:** Beg with a p row, work
11 rows in st-st.

**Row 26:** (K2tog) to end (10 sts).

**Row 27:** Purl.

**Row 28:** (K2tog) to end (5 sts).

Thread yarn through sts on needle,
pull tight and secure by threading yarn
a second time through sts.

### Arms for Baby Bear (make 2)

Beg at shoulder, using the thumb method and G, cast on 4 sts.

**Row 1 (WS):** Purl.

**Row 2:** K1, m1, k to last st, m1, k1 (6 sts).

**Rows 3 to 12:** Rep rows 1 and 2, 5 times more (16 sts).

**Rows 13 to 17:** Beg with a p row, work 5 rows in st-st.

**Row 18:** (K2tog) to end (8 sts).

**Row 19:** (P2tog) to end (4 sts).

Thread yarn through sts on needle, pull tight and secure by threading yarn a second time through sts.

### Ears
### Ears for Father Bear (make 2)

Beg at lower edge, using the thumb method and G, cast on 28 sts, WS facing to beg.

**Rows 1 to 3:** Beg with a p row, work 3 rows in st-st.

**Row 4:** (K5, k2tog, k2tog, k5) twice (24 sts).

**Row 5 and foll 3 alt rows:** Purl.

**Row 6:** (K4, k2tog, k2tog, k4) twice (20 sts).

**Row 8:** (K3, k2tog, k2tog, k3) twice (16 sts).

**Row 10:** (K2, k2tog, k2tog, k2) twice (12 sts).

**Row 12:** (K1, k2tog, k2tog, k1) twice (8 sts).

**Row 13:** (P2tog) to end (4 sts).

Thread yarn through sts on needle, pull tight and secure by threading yarn a second time through sts.

### Ears for Mother Bear (make 2)

Beg at lower edge, using the thumb method and G, cast on 20 sts, WS facing to beg.

**Rows 1 to 3:** Beg with a p row, work 3 rows in st-st.

**Row 4:** (K3, k2tog, k2tog, k3) twice (16 sts).

**Row 5 and foll alt row:** Purl.

**Row 6:** (K2, k2tog, k2tog, k2) twice (12 sts).

**Row 8:** (K1, k2tog, k2tog, k1) twice (8 sts).

**Row 9:** (P2tog) to end (4 sts).

Thread yarn through sts on needle, pull tight and secure by threading yarn a second time through sts.

### Ears for Baby Bear (make 2)

Beg at lower edge, using the thumb method and G, cast on 12 sts, WS facing to beg.

**Rows 1 to 3:** Beg with a p row, work 3 rows in st-st.

**Row 4:** (K1, k2tog, k2tog, k1) twice (8 sts).

**Row 5:** (P2tog) to end (4 sts).

Thread yarn through sts on needle, pull tight and secure by threading yarn a second time through sts.

## Clothes for Bears
### Cap for Father Bear

Using the thumb method and H, cast on 44 sts, RS facing to beg.

**Rows 1 and 2:** K 1 row then p 1 row.

**Row 3:** K2, (m1, k2) to end (65 sts).

**Rows 4 to 10:** Beg with a p row, work 7 rows in st-st.

**Row 11:** K1, (k2tog, k6) to end (57 sts).

**Row 12 and foll 5 alt rows:** Purl.

**Row 13:** K1, (k2tog, k5) to end (49 sts).

**Row 15:** K1, (k2tog, k4) to end (41 sts).

**Row 17:** K1, (k2tog, k3) to end (33 sts).

**Row 19:** K1, (k2tog, k2) to end (25 sts).

**Row 21:** K1, (k2tog, k1) to end (17 sts).

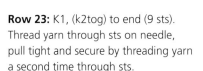

**Row 23:** K1, (k2tog) to end (9 sts).
Thread yarn through sts on needle,
pull tight and secure by threading yarn
a second time through sts.

**Peak**

Using the thumb method and H, cast on
15 sts, WS facing to beg.

**Rows 1 to 3:** Beg with a p row, work
3 rows in st-st.

**Row 4:** K2tog, k to last 2 sts, k2tog (13 sts).

**Row 5:** Purl.

**Row 6:** K1, m1, k to last st, m1, k1 (15 sts).

**Rows 7 to 9:** Beg with a p row, work 3
rows in st-st.
Cast off.

**Dungarees for Father Bear**

**Front of dungarees**

**First leg**

Using the thumb method and I, cast on
19 sts and beg in g-st, RS facing to beg.

**Rows 1 and 2:** Work 2 rows in g-st.

**Rows 3 to 12:** Beg with a k row, work
10 rows in st-st.
Break yarn and set aside.

**Second leg**

Work as first leg but do not break yarn.

**Join legs**

**Row 13:** K across sts of second leg, turn
and cast on 5 sts, turn and cont k across
sts of first leg (43 sts).

**Rows 14 to 32:** Beg with a p row, work
19 rows in st-st.

**Rows 33 to 35:** Work 3 rows in g-st,
ending with a RS row. **

**Shape bib**

**Row 36:** Cast off 12 sts kwise, k18 (19 sts
now on RH needle), cast off rem 12 sts,
fasten off and rejoin yarn to rem sts (19 sts).

**Row 37:** Knit.

**Row 38:** K2, p to last 2 sts, k2.

**Rows 39 to 52:** Rep rows 37 and 38,
7 times more.

**Rows 53 to 55:** Work 3 rows in g-st
ending with a RS row.
Cast off in g-st.

**Back of dungarees**

Work as front from beg to **.
Cast off all sts in g-st.

**Straps (make 2)**

Using the thumb method and I, cast on 40
sts and work in g-st.

**Row 1 (RS):** Knit.
Cast off in g-st.

**Pinafore for Mother Bear**

**Front of pinafore**

Using the thumb method and J, cast on 44
sts and beg in g-st, RS facing to beg.

**Rows 1 and 2:** Work 2 rows in g-st.

**Rows 3 to 20:** Beg with a k row, work 18
rows in st-st.

**Row 21:** K1, k2tog, (k2, k2tog) to last st,
k1 (33 sts).

**Rows 22 and 23:** Work 2 rows in g-st. **

**Shape bib**

**Row 24:** Cast off 9 sts kwise, k14 (15 sts
now on RH needle), cast off rem 9 sts,
fasten off and rejoin yarn to rem sts (15 sts).

**Row 25:** Knit.

**Row 26:** K2, p to last 2 sts, k2.

**Rows 27 to 36:** Rep rows 23 and 24, 5
times more.

**Rows 37 to 39:** Work 3 rows in g-st
ending with a RS row.
Cast off in g-st.

**Back of Pinafore**

Work as front from beg to **.
Cast off all sts in g-st.

**Straps (make 2)**

Using the thumb method and J, cast on 30
sts and work in g-st.

**Row 1 (RS):** Knit.
Cast off in g-st.

**Dungarees for Baby Bear**

**Front of dungarees**

**First leg**

Using the thumb method and K, cast on
12 sts and beg in g-st, RS facing to beg.

**Rows 1 and 2:** Work 2 rows in g-st.

**Rows 3 and 4:** Beg with a k row, work
2 rows in st-st.
Break yarn and set aside.

**Second leg**

Work as first leg but do not break yarn.

**Join legs**

**Row 5:** K across sts of second leg, turn
and cast on 2 sts, turn and cont k across
sts of first leg (26 sts).

**Rows 6 to 10:** Beg with a p row, work
5 rows in st-st.

**Rows 11 to 13:** Work 3 rows in g-st,
ending with a RS row. **

**Shape bib**

**Row 14:** Cast off 8 sts kwise, k9 (10 sts
now on RH needle), cast off rem 8 sts,
fasten off and rejoin yarn to rem sts
(10 sts).

**Row 15:** Knit.

**Row 16:** K2, p to last 2 sts, k2.

**Rows 17 to 22:** Rep rows 15 and 16,
3 times more.

**Rows 23 to 25:** Work 3 rows in g-st
ending with a RS row.
Cast off in g-st.

**Back of dungarees**

Work as front from beg to **.
Cast off all sts in g-st.

**Straps (make 2)**

Using the thumb method and K, cast on
25 sts and work in g-st.

**Row 1 (RS):** Knit.
Cast off in g-st.

# Making up Bears

### Body for Three Bears
Place wrong sides of two pieces of body together, matching all edges. Leaving neck open, work mattress stitch around outside edge. Stuff legs and body.

### Head for Three Bears
Fold cast-off stitches at top of nose in half and oversew. Sew up row ends of head, stuff head and place a ball of stuffing into nose. Pin and sew head to body by taking a short horizontal stitch from head, and then a short horizontal stitch from body, and do this alternately all the way round leaving a gap. Add stuffing to neck and sew up gap.

### Arms for Three Bears
Sew up straight row ends of arms and stuff. Leaving armholes open, sew arms to Bears, sewing top of arms to neck.

### Ears for Three Bears
Sew up row ends of ears and with this seam at centre back, pin and sew ears to Mother Bear and Baby Bear. Sew Father Bear's ears on after sewing his cap on.

### Cap for Father Bear
Sew up row ends of cap and stuff lightly. Pin and sew lower edge of cap to head. Fold peak bringing cast-on and cast-off stitches together and sew up and sew peak to lower edge of cap at centre front.

### Features
Embroider features in black: mark position of eyes with two pins and work a vertical chain stitch for each eye and then a second chain stitch on top of first chain stitch for Father and Mother Bear, and a single chain stitch for Baby Bear. Embroider nose and mouth using straight stitches (see page 171 for how to begin and fasten off the embroidery invisibly).

### Dungarees and straps
Sew up row ends of legs of dungarees and across crotch. Place dungarees on Bears and sew straps to bib, take straps over shoulders, cross over and sew to waist of dungarees at back. Sew cast-off stitches of dungarees to Bears.

### Pinafore and straps
Sew up row ends of skirt of pinafore. Place pinafore on Bear and sew straps to bib, take straps over shoulders, cross over and sew to waist of pinafore at back. Sew cast-off stitches of pinafore to Bear.

# How to make Bowls of Porridge and Spoons

### Big bowl

Beg at centre of base of bowl, using the thumb method and L, cast on 10 sts, WS facing to beg.

**Row 1 and foll 3 alt rows:** Purl.
**Row 2:** K1, (m1, k1) to end (19 sts).
**Row 4:** K1, (m1, k2) to end (28 sts).
**Row 6:** K1, (m1, k3) to end (37 sts).
**Row 8:** K1, (m1, k4) to end (46 sts).
**Rows 9 to 17:** Beg with a p row, work 9 rows in st-st.
**Rows 18 to 25:** Change to C and work 8 rows in g-st.
**Rows 26 to 33:** Beg with a k row, work 8 rows in st-st.
**Row 34:** K1, (k2tog, k3) to end (37 sts).
**Row 35 and foll 2 alt rows:** Purl.
**Row 36:** K1, (k2tog, k2) to end (28 sts).
**Row 38:** K1, (k2tog, k1) to end (19 sts).
**Row 40:** K1, (k2tog) to end (10 sts).
Thread yarn through sts on needle, pull tight and secure by threading yarn a second time through sts.

### Porridge

Using the thumb method and M, cast on 7 sts and work in moss-st, RS facing to beg.

**Row 1:** K1, (p1, k1) to end (this row will be referred to as moss-st).
**Row 2:** K1, (p1, k1, p1) into front of next st, k1, p1, k1, (p1, k1, p1) into front of next st, k1 (11 sts).
**Row 3:** Work 1 row in moss-st.
**Row 4:** K1, (p1, k1, p1) into front of next st, moss-st 7 sts, (p1, k1, p1) into front of next st, k1 (15 sts).
**Rows 5 to 16:** Work 12 rows in moss-st.
**Row 17:** K1, p3tog, moss-st 7 sts, p3tog, k1 (11 sts).
**Row 18:** Work 1 row in moss-st.
**Row 19:** K1, p3tog, k1, p1, k1, p3tog, k1 (7 sts).
**Row 20:** Work 1 row in moss-st.
Cast off in moss-st.

### Medium bowl

Beg at centre of base of bowl, using the thumb method and L, cast on 10 sts, WS facing to beg.

**Row 1 and foll 2 alt rows:** Purl.
**Row 2:** K1, (m1, k1) to end (19 sts).
**Row 4:** K1, (m1, k2) to end (28 sts).
**Row 6:** K1, (m1, k3) to end (37 sts).
**Rows 7 to 13:** Beg with a p row, work 7 rows in st-st.
**Rows 14 to 21:** Change to C and work 8 rows in g-st.
**Rows 22 to 27:** Beg with a k row, work 6 rows in st-st.
**Row 28:** K1, (k2tog, k2) to end (28 sts).
**Row 29 and foll alt row:** Purl.
**Row 30:** K1, (k2tog, k1) to end (19 sts).
**Row 32:** K1, (k2tog) to end (10 sts).
Thread yarn through sts on needle, pull tight and secure by threading yarn a second time through sts.

## Porridge

Using the thumb method and M, cast on 7 sts and work in moss-st, RS facing to beg.

**Row 1:** K1, (p1, k1) to end (this row will be referred to as moss-st).

**Row 2:** K1, (p1, k1, p1) into front of next st, k1, p1, k1, (p1, k1, p1) into front of next st, k1 (11 sts).

**Rows 3 to 12:** Work 10 rows in moss-st.

**Row 13:** K1, p3tog, k1, p1, k1, p3tog, k1 (7 sts).

**Row 14:** Work 1 row in moss-st.

Cast off in moss-st.

## Small bowl

Beg at centre of base of bowl, using the thumb method and L, cast on 9 sts, WS facing to beg.

**Row 1 and foll alt row:** Purl.

**Row 2:** K1, (m1, k1) to end (17 sts).

**Row 4:** K1, (m1, k2) to end (25 sts).

**Rows 5 to 9:** Beg with a p row, work 5 rows in st-st.

**Rows 10 to 15:** Change to C and work 6 rows in g-st.

**Rows 16 to 19:** Beg with a k row, work 4 rows in st-st.

**Row 20:** K1, (k2tog, k1) to end (17 sts).

**Row 21:** Purl.

**Row 22:** K1, (k2tog) to end (9 sts).

Thread yarn through sts on needle, pull tight and secure by threading yarn a second time through sts.

## Porridge

Using the thumb method and M, cast on 5 sts and work in moss-st, RS facing to beg.

**Row 1:** K1, (p1, k1) to end (this row will be referred to as moss-st).

**Row 2:** K1, (p1, k1, p1) into front of next st, k1, (p1, k1, p1) into front of next st, k1 (9 sts).

**Rows 3 to 6:** Work 4 rows in moss-st.

**Row 7:** K1, p3tog, k1, p3tog, k1 (5 sts).

**Row 8:** Work 1 row in moss-st.

Cast off in moss-st.

## Big spoon

Using the thumb method and N, cast on 24 sts.

**Row 1 (WS):** S1p, p8, turn,

**Row 2:** S1k, k to end.

**Row 3:** S1p, p9.

**Row 4:** S1k, k to end.

**Rows 5 and 6:** Rep rows 3 and 4.

**Row 7:** S1p, p8, turn.

**Row 8:** S1k, k to end.

**Rows 9 to 12:** Beg with a p row, work 4 rows in st-st.

**Rows 13 and 14:** Rep rows 7 and 8.

**Rows 15 to 18:** Rep rows 3 to 6.

**Rows 19 and 20:** Rep rows 1 and 2.

**Row 21:** Purl.

Cast off loosely.

## Medium spoon

Using the thumb method and N, cast on 18 sts.

**Row 1 (WS):** S1p, p6, turn,

**Row 2:** S1k, k to end.

**Row 3:** S1p, p7.

**Row 4:** S1k, k to end.

**Row 5:** S1p, p6, turn.

**Row 6:** S1k, k to end.

**Rows 7 to 10:** Beg with a p row, work 4 rows in st-st.

**Rows 11 and 12:** Rep rows 5 and 6.

**Rows 13 and 14:** Rep rows 3 and 4.

**Rows 15 and 16:** Rep rows 1 and 2.

**Row 17:** Purl.

Cast off loosely.

## Small spoon

Using the thumb method and N, cast on 12 sts.

**Row 1 (WS):** S1p, p4, turn,

**Row 2:** S1k, k to end.

**Row 3:** S1p, p5, turn.

**Row 4:** S1k, k to end.

**Row 5:** Purl across all sts.

**Row 6:** Knit.

**Rows 7 and 8:** Rep rows 3 and 4.

**Rows 9 and 10:** Rep rows 1 and 2.

**Row 11:** Purl.

Cast off loosely.

# Making up Bowls of Porridge and Spoons

## Bowls and porridge

With right sides of stocking stitch outside, sew up row ends of Bowls. Assemble lining in inside of Bowls and sew through centre to secure. Place a small ball of stuffing into Bowls and sew outer edge of porridge to Bowl, leaving a gap. Add more stuffing and sew up gap.

## Spoons

With right side of stocking stitch outside, sew up cast-on and cast-off stitches of bowl of Spoon; this seam will be at centre back. Fold chenille stick in half, insert into wrong side of handle of Spoon and sew up cast-on and cast-off stitches of handle around chenille stick. Trim excess chenille stick and gather round row ends and top and bottom of Spoon, pull tight and secure. To shape bowl of Spoon, sew a gathering stitch round outside edge of bowl of Spoon, pull to curve and fasten off.

Once upon a time, a king and queen had a beautiful baby girl. They thought they had invited all the fairies in the kingdom to her christening, but unfortunately they had forgotten one, who was also a bit of a witch. Out of spite, she put a curse on the princess...

# SLEEPING BEAUTY

# Information you'll need

### Finished size
Sleeping Beauty measures 8½in (22cm) high
Bed measures 10in (25cm) long
Prince measures 8½in (22cm) high

### Materials
**Any DK (US: light worsted) yarn**
**Note:** amounts are approximate
30g white (A)
30g red (B)
10g pale pink (C)
10g brown (D)
5g lemon (E)
150g mauve (F)
30g green (G)
5g black (H)
5g grey (I)
15g medium blue (J)
20g gold (K)
5g dark brown (L)
5g bright green (M)
Oddments of black, red and pale pink
for embroidery
1 pair of 3.25mm (UK10:US3) needles
and a spare needle of the same size
Knitters' blunt-ended pins and a needle
for sewing up
Tweezers for stuffing small parts (optional)
Acrylic toy stuffing
Red pencil for shading cheeks

### Tension
26 sts x 34 rows measure 4in (10cm)
square over st-st using 3.25mm needles
and DK yarn before stuffing.

### Working instructions
Sew up all row-end seams on right side
using mattress stitch, unless otherwise
stated; a one-stitch seam allowance has
been allowed for this.

# How to make Sleeping Beauty

**Note:** Sleeping Beauty is a topsy-turvy doll – one way up she is asleep, the other way up she is awake.

## Bodices and heads
### (Make 2 pieces: one bodice in A for asleep end and one bodice in B for awake end)

Using the thumb method and A or B for bodice, cast on 28 sts, WS facing to beg.

**Rows 1 to 13:** Beg with a p row, work 13 rows in st-st.

**Rows 14 and 15:** Change to C for head and work 2 rows in st-st.

**Row 16:** *K4, (m1, k2) 4 times, k2; rep from * once (36 sts).

**Rows 17 to 31:** Beg with a p row, work 15 rows in st-st.

**Shape top of head**

**Row 32:** (K2tog, k2) to end (27 sts).

**Row 33 and foll alt row:** Purl.

**Row 34:** (K2tog, k1) to end (18 sts).

**Row 36:** (K2tog) to end (9 sts).

Thread yarn through sts on needle, pull tight and secure by threading yarn a second time through sts.

## Skirts of dresses
### Skirt for asleep doll

Beg at lower edge of skirt of dress, using the thumb method and B, cast on 72 sts and beg in g-st, RS facing to beg.

**Rows 1 to 4:** Work 4 rows in g-st.

**Rows 5 and 6:** K 1 row, then p 1 row.

**Rows 7 and 8:** Work 2 rows in g-st.

**Rows 9 to 16:** Rep rows 5 to 8 twice more.

**Rows 17 to 30:** Change to A and beg with a k row, work 14 rows in st-st.

**Row 31:** (K2tog, k4) to end (60 sts).

**Rows 32 to 34:** Beg with a p row, work 3 rows in st-st.

**Row 35:** (K2tog, k3) to end (48 sts).

**Rows 36 to 38:** Beg with a p row, work 3 rows in st-st.

**Row 39:** (K2tog, k2) to end (36 sts). Cast off pwise.

### Skirt for awake doll

Beg at lower edge of skirt of dress, using the thumb method and A, cast on 72 sts, WS facing to beg.

**Rows 1 to 8:** Beg with a p row, work 8 rows in st-st, ending with a RS row (this part is turned under).

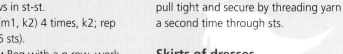

**Picot row:** K2, (yf, k2tog) to end.
**Rows 10 to 17:** Beg with a k row, work 8 rows in st-st.
**Rows 18 to 21:** Change to B and work 4 rows in g-st.
**Rows 22 to 41:** Beg with a k row, work 20 rows in st-st.
**Row 42:** (K2tog, k4) to end (60 sts).
**Rows 43 to 45:** Beg with a p row, work 3 rows in st-st.
**Row 46:** (K2tog, k3) to end (48 sts).
**Rows 47 to 49:** Beg with a p row, work 3 rows in st-st.
**Row 50:** (K2tog, k2) to end (36 sts). Cast off pwise.

## Sash (make 1 for awake end)

Using the thumb method and A, cast on 36 sts.
**Row 1 (RS):** Knit.
Cast off kwise.

## Sleeves and hands
## (make 2 sleeves in A for asleep end and 2 sleeves in B for awake end)

Beg at sleeve, using the thumb method and A or B, cast on 9 sts.
**Row 1 (WS):** Purl.
**Row 2:** (K2, m1) twice, k1, (m1, k2) twice (13 sts).
**Rows 3 to 17:** Beg with a p row, work 15 rows in st-st.
**Row 18:** K3, (k2tog, k3) twice (11 sts).
**Rows 19 to 23:** Change to C for hand and beg with a p row, work 5 rows in st-st.
**Row 24:** K2tog, (k1, k2tog) to end (7 sts). Thread yarn through sts on needle, pull tight and secure by threading yarn a second time through sts.

## Cuffs
## (make 2 in B for asleep end and 2 in A for awake end)

Using the thumb method and A or B, cast on 15 sts, RS facing to beg.
Cast off pwise.

## Hair (make 2 pieces alike)

Make hair as for Jack's Mother on page 45, using D.

## Hair loops
## (make 4 for awake end)

Using the thumb method and D, cast on 16 sts, RS facing to beg.
Cast off loosely, pwise.

## Crown

Make crown for awake end as crown for Prince in Cinderella on page 79, using E.

## Making up Sleeping Beauty

### Bodices and heads

Sew up row ends of both heads and bodices and stuff. Matching seams, place lower edges of bodices together and oversew, leaving a gap. Add more stuffing and sew up gap. To shape necks, take a double length of yarn in colour to match bodice and sew a running stitch round last row of upper body, sewing in and out of every half stitch. Pull tight, knot yarn and sew ends into neck.

### Skirts of dresses

Sew up row ends of skirt of dress for asleep end. With seam at centre back, place skirt of dress for asleep end on doll and sew cast-off stitches at waist to first row of white bodice. Fold skirt for awake end along picot edge and sew cast-on stitches in place. Turn doll the other way up, pulling skirt down to lower edge. Sew up row ends of skirt for awake end from lower edge to 2in (5cm) below waist.

Place skirt on doll for awake end and finish sewing up row ends. With seam at centre back, sew cast-off stitches at waist to first row of red bodice.

## Sash

Place sash around waist of awake end and oversew row ends. Sew sash to waist of doll all the way round.

## Sleeves and hands

Sew up row ends of hands and place a small ball of stuffing into hands. Sew up row ends of sleeves from wrist to 1in (2.5cm) below shoulder. Stuff sleeves and finish sewing up row ends. With seam at centre of inside edge, sew across cast-on stitches. Sew cast-on stitches of the four arms to second row below neck at each side by oversewing.

## Cuffs

Place cuffs around four wrists and sew up row ends. Sew cuffs to wrists using back stitch down centre of cuff all the way round.

## Features

Work features for awake end as for Jack's Mother on page 46. For asleep end, and using picture as a guide, embroider two closed eyes in black using straight stitches. Embroider nose and a very shallow 'v' for mouth as for Jack's Mother on page 46.

## Hair

Make up hair as for Jack's Mother on page 46. Repeat for other end.

## Plaits for asleep doll

Make a plait in colour to match hair by cutting nine lengths of yarn, each 20in (50cm) long, and lay them in a bundle. Tie a knot at centre of bundle and fold in half. Divide into three and plait for 2in (5cm) and tie a knot. Trim ends beyond knot to ½in (13mm). Repeat for second plait and sew plaits to hair at sides of head.

## Hair loops for awake doll

Oversew row ends of each hair loop and sew two hair loops to each side of hair.

# How to make Bed

Make bed and pillow as for Grandma's Bed in Little Red Riding Hood on pages 124–5, using F throughout for bed and G for pillow.

## Eiderdown

Using the thumb method and G, cast on 36 sts and work in g-st, RS facing to beg.

**Rows 1 to 4:** Work 4 rows in g-st.

**Rows 5 to 10:** Join in F and work 6 rows in g-st.

**Rows 11 to 16:** Carrying yarn loosely up side of work and using G, work 6 rows in g-st.

**Rows 17 to 28:** Rep rows 5 to 16 once.

**Rows 29 and 30:** Change to F, cont in g-st and using the knitting-on method, cast on 10 sts at beg of next 2 rows (56 sts).

**Rows 31 to 34:** Using F, work 4 rows in g-st.

**Rows 35 to 40:** Using G, work 6 rows in g-st.

**Rows 41 to 46:** Using F, work 6 rows in g-st.

**Rows 47 to 106:** Rep rows 35 to 46, 5 times more.

**Rows 107 to 111:** Using G, work 5 rows in g-st.

Cast off in g-st.

## Edging

Work edging along row ends of wide part and with RS facing and using G, pick up and knit 42 sts along edge.

**Rows 1 to 4:** Work 4 rows in g-st.

Cast off in g-st.

Rep for opposite edge.

# Making up Bed

## Bed and pillow

Make up Bed and Pillow as for Grandma's Bed and Pillow on page 125.

## Eiderdown

Sew up corner seams and row ends of edging at bottom edge.

# How to make Prince

## Shoes, legs, body and head

Make shoes, legs, body and head as for Cinderella in Rags on page 73, using H for shoes, A for legs, I for lower body, J for upper body and C for head.

## Breeches and tunic

Make breeches and tunic as for Prince in Cinderella on page 78, using J for breeches, beg in K and change to J for tunic.

## Sleeves, hands and hair

Make sleeves, hands and hair as for Jack's Mother on page 45, using J for sleeves, C for hands and L for hair.

## Cuffs, collar of cloak, cloak and brooch

Make cuffs, collar, of cloak, cloak and brooch as for Prince in Cinderella on pages 78–9, using K for cuffs, collar of cloak and cloak and B for brooch.

## Hat

Beg at brim, using the thumb method and J, cast on 64 sts and beg in g-st, RS facing to beg.

**Rows 1 and 2:** Work 2 rows in g-st.
**Row 3:** K24, (k2tog, k2) to end (54 sts).
**Rows 4 to 6:** Work 3 rows in g-st.
**Row 7:** (K2tog, k1) to end (36 sts).
**Rows 8 to 14:** Beg with a p row, work 7 rows in st-st.
**Row 15:** (K2tog, k2) to end (27 sts).
**Row 16 and foll alt row:** Purl.
**Row 17:** (K2tog, k1) to end (18 sts).
**Row 19:** (K2tog) to end (9 sts).
Thread yarn through sts on needle, pull tight and secure by threading yarn a second time through sts.

## Feathers (make one in each of B, K and M)

Using the thumb method and B, K or M, cast on 18 sts.
**Row 1 (RS):** K6, (k3tog) twice, k6 (14 sts).
Cast off kwise.

# Making up Prince

## Shoes, legs, body and head

Make up shoes, legs, body and head as for Cinderella in Rags on page 73.

## Breeches and tunic

Make up breeches and tunic as for Prince in Cinderella on page 79.

## Sleeves, hands, features and hair

Make up sleeves, hands and hair and work features as for Jack's Mother on pages 45–6.

## Cuffs, collar of cloak, cloak and brooch

Make up cuffs, collar of cloak, cloak and brooch as for Prince in Cinderella on page 79.

## Hat and feathers

Sew up row ends of hat and oversew row ends of brim. Lightly stuff top of hat and place hat on head. With seam at right-hand side, pin and sew hat to head using back stitch on right side of base of brim, sewing through hat to head. Fold cast-off stitches of feathers in half and oversew. Using picture as a guide, sew feathers to hat, turn up brim and sew in place.

Hansel and Gretel lived with their father, who was a woodcutter, and their stepmother, who was very cruel. One day, their stepmother took them into the forest and left them there. Hansel and Gretel, lost and scared, wandered deeper and deeper into the forest until they saw a house made of gingerbread, sweets and icing...

# HANSEL & GRETEL

# Information you'll need

## Finished size
Hansel and Gretel measure 6½in
(16.5cm) high
Gingerbread house measures 10in
(25cm) high

## Materials
**Any DK (US: light worsted) yarn**
**Note:** amounts are approximate
5g black (A)
10g pale pink (B)
5g grey (C)
15g white (D)
10g mustard (E)
5g beige (F)
5g brown (G)
5g dark brown (H)
10g purple (I)
5g pale brown (J)
5g blue (K)
5g green (L)
125g ginger (M)
10g bright pink (N)
Oddments of black, red and pale pink
for embroidery
1 pair of 3.25mm (UK10:US3) needles
and a spare needle of the same size
Knitters' blunt-ended pins and a needle
for sewing up
Tweezers for stuffing small parts (optional)
Acrylic toy stuffing
Red pencil for shading cheeks

## Tension
26 sts x 34 rows measure 4in (10cm)
square over st-st using 3.25mm needles
and DK yarn before stuffing.

## Working instructions
Sew up all row-end seams on right side
using mattress stitch, unless otherwise
stated; a one-stitch seam allowance has
been allowed for this.

# How to make Hansel

## Shoes, legs, body and head

Make shoes, legs, body and head as for Courtier in Cinderella on page 80, using A for shoes, B for legs, C for lower body, D for upper body and B for head.

## Breeches and belt
### First leg
Beg at lower edge, using the thumb method and E, cast on 18 sts, RS facing to beg.

**Rows 1 to 12:** Beg with a k row, work 12 rows in st-st.

**Rows 13 and 14:** Work 2 rows in st-st and cast off 1 st at beg of these 2 rows (16 sts).

Break yarn and set aside.

### Second leg
Work as first leg but do not break yarn.

### Join legs
**Row 15:** With RS facing, k across sts of second leg, and then with the same yarn cont k across sts of first leg (32 sts).

**Rows 16 to 20:** Beg with a p row, work 5 rows in st-st.

### Work belt
**Rows 21 and 22:** Work 2 rows in g-st. Cast off pwise.

## Sleeves and hands
Make sleeves and hands as for Jack on page 41, using D for sleeves and B for hands.

## Braces (make 2)
Using the thumb method and F, cast on 24 sts, RS facing to beg.
Cast off pwise.

## Hair
Make hair as for Jack on page 42, using G.

# Making up Hansel

## Shoes, legs, body and head
Make up shoes, legs, body and head as for Courtier in Cinderella on page 81.

## Breeches
Sew up leg seams of breeches from lower edge to crotch. Sew round crotch by oversewing and sew up row ends at centre back. Place breeches on doll and sew cast-off stitches of waist of breeches to first row of upper body all the way round.

## Sleeves and hands
Make up sleeves and hands as for Jack on page 43.

## Braces
Sew ends of braces to breeches at front, take over shoulders, cross over and sew to breeches at back.

## Features and hair
Work features and make up hair as for Jack on page 43.

# How to make Gretel

## Shoes, legs, body and head

Make shoes, legs, body and head as for
Courtier in Cinderella on page 80, using
H for shoes, B for legs, D for lower body,
I for upper body and B for head.

## Skirt of dress

Beg at lower edge, using the thumb
method and I, cast on 50 sts and beg
in g-st, RS facing to beg.
**Rows 1 to 4:** Work 4 rows in g-st.
**Rows 5 to 18:** Beg with a k row, work
14 rows in st-st.
**Row 19:** (K2tog, k3) to end (40 sts).
**Rows 20 to 22:** Beg with a p row, work
3 rows in st-st.
**Row 23:** (K2tog, k2) to end (30 sts).
Cast off kwise.

## Sleeves and hands

Make sleeves and hands as for Jack on
page 41, using I for sleeve and B for hand.

## Hair

Make hair as for Jack on page 42, using J.

## Patches

**Note:** make one patch in K and one patch
in L.
Using the thumb method and K or L, cast
on 4 sts and work in g-st, RS facing to beg.
**Rows 1 to 3:** Work 3 rows in g-st.
Cast off in g-st.

# Making up Gretel

## Shoes, legs, body and head

Make up shoes, legs, body and head as for
Courtier in Cinderella on page 81.

## Skirt of dress

Sew up row ends of skirt of dress, place
on doll and sew cast-off stitches to first
row of upper body all the way round.

## Sleeves and hands

Make up sleeves and hands as for Jack
on page 43.

## Features

Work features as for Jack on page 43.

## Hair and plaits

Make up hair and plaits as for Princess in
The Princess and the Pea on page 114.

## Patches

Sew patches onto skirt.

# How to make Gingerbread House

## Front and back (make 2 pieces)

Using the thumb method and M, cast on 45 sts, WS facing to beg.

**Rows 1 to 45:** Beg with a p row, work 45 rows in st-st.

**Row 46:** K2tog, k to last 2 sts, k2tog (43 sts).

**Row 47:** Purl.

**Rows 48 to 87:** Rep rows 46 and 47, 20 times more (3 sts).

**Row 88:** K3tog tbl (1 st).

Fasten off.

## Sides (make 2 pieces)

Using the thumb method and M, cast on 30 sts, WS facing to beg.

**Rows 1 to 45:** Beg with a p row, work 45 rows in st-st.

Cast off.

## Door

Using the thumb method and N, cast on 12 sts, WS facing to beg.

**Rows 1 to 25:** Beg with a p row, work 25 rows in st-st.

**Rows 26 to 30:** Change to D and work 5 rows in g-st.

Cast off in g-st.

### Side pieces of door (make 2 pieces)

Using the thumb method and D, cast on 21 sts and work in g-st.

**Rows 1 to 3:** Work 3 rows in g-st.

Cast off in g-st.

## Door handle

Using the thumb method and M, cast on 9 sts.

**Row 1 (WS):** Purl.

Thread yarn through sts on needle, pull tight and secure by threading yarn a second time through sts.

## Small windows (make 5)

Using the thumb method and N, cast on 8 sts and beg in g-st, RS facing to beg.

**Rows 1 and 2:** Work 2 rows in g-st.

**Rows 3 to 10:** Change to D and beg with a k row, work 8 rows in st-st.

**Rows 11 to 13:** Change to N and work 3 rows in g-st.

Cast off in g-st.

### Side pieces of windows (make 10 pieces)

Using the thumb method and N, cast on 10 sts and work in g-st.

**Row 1 (RS):** Knit.

Cast off in g-st.

## Making up Gingerbread House

### Long window
Using the thumb method and N, cast on 24 sts and beg in g-st, RS facing to beg.
**Rows 1 and 2:** Work 2 rows in g-st.
**Rows 3 to 10:** Change to D and beg with a k row, work 8 rows in st-st.
**Rows 11 to 13:** Change to N and work 3 rows in g-st.
Cast off in g-st.
### Side pieces of window (make 2 pieces)
Using the thumb method and N, cast on 10 sts and work in g-st.
**Row 1 (RS):** Knit.
Cast off in g-st.

### Roof (make 2 pieces)
Using the thumb method and M, cast on 30 sts and work in g-st, RS facing to beg.
**Rows 1 to 75:** Work 75 rows in g-st.
Cast off in g-st.

### Base
Using the thumb method and M, cast on 45 sts, WS facing to beg.
**Rows 1 to 51:** Beg with a p row, work 51 rows in st-st.
Cast off.

### Front, back and sides
Sew row ends of side pieces to front and back.

### Door and windows
Using picture as a guide, sew door to centre front, sewing around outside edge, and sew side pieces of door to sides. Sew handle to door. Sew a window at each side of door, the long window above and another small window above this, and sew side pieces of windows to sides. Sew a small window to each side of Gingerbread House likewise.

### Roof
Oversew cast-off stitches of both roof pieces together. Pin and sew roof to Gingerbread House. Stuff Gingerbread House with plenty of stuffing.

### Base
Sew base to Gingerbread House around outside edge, leaving a gap. Adjust stuffing, adding more, and sew up gap.

An old woman once decided to bake a gingerbread man. She gave him an icing-sugar mouth, a cherry nose and used currents for buttons and eyes. Then she put him in the oven to bake. When he was done, she carefully opened the oven door and out he ran...

# THE GINGERBREAD MAN

# Information you'll need

### Finished size
The Gingerbread Man measures 11in (28cm) high

### Materials
**Any DK (US: light worsted) yarn**
**Note:** amounts are approximate
50g ginger (A)
Oddments of black, red and white for embroidery
1 pair of 3.25mm (UK10:US3) needles and a spare needle of the same size
Knitters' blunt-ended pins and a needle for sewing up
Acrylic toy stuffing

### Tension
26 sts x 34 rows measure 4in (10cm) square over st-st using 3.25mm needles and DK yarn before stuffing.

### Working instructions
Sew up all row-end seams on right side using mattress stitch; a one-stitch seam allowance has been allowed for this.

# How to make The Gingerbread Man

## Body and head (make 2 pieces)

### First leg

Beg at lower edge, using the thumb method and A, cast on 5 sts.

**Row 1 (WS):** Purl.

**Row 2:** K1, (m1, k1) to end (9 sts).

**Row 3:** Purl.

**Row 4:** K1, m1, k to last st, m1, k1 (11 sts).

**Rows 5 to 8:** Rep rows 3 and 4, twice more (15 sts).

**Rows 9 to 29:** Beg with a p row, work 21 rows in st-st.

Break yarn and set aside.

### Second leg

Work as first leg but do not break yarn.

### Join legs

**Row 30:** With RS facing, k across sts of second leg, turn, and using the knitting-on method, cast on 5 sts, turn, and with the same yarn cont k across sts of first leg (35 sts).

**Rows 31 to 33:** Beg with a p row, work 3 rows in st-st.

**Row 34:** K16, k3tog, k16 (33 sts).

**Rows 35 to 37:** Beg with a p row, work 3 rows in st-st.

**Row 38:** K15, k3tog, k15 (31 sts).

**Rows 39 to 41:** Beg with a p row, work 3 rows in st-st.

**Row 42:** K14, k3tog, k14 (29 sts).

**Rows 43 to 45:** Beg with a p row, work 3 rows in st-st.

**Row 46:** K13, k3tog, k13 (27 sts).

**Rows 47 to 49:** Beg with a p row, work 3 rows in st-st.

**Row 50:** K1, m1, k11, k3tog, k11, m1, k1 (27 sts).

**Row 51:** Purl.

**Rows 52 and 53:** Work 2 rows in st-st and using the knitting-on method, cast on 10 sts at beg of these 2 rows (47 sts).

**Row 54:** K1, m1, k to last st, m1, k1 (49 sts).

**Row 55:** Purl.

**Row 56:** As row 54 (51 sts).

**Rows 57 to 63:** Beg with a p row, work 7 rows in st-st.

**Row 64:** K2tog, k to last 2 sts, k2tog (49 sts).

**Row 65:** Purl.

**Rows 66 and 67:** Rep rows 64 and 65 once (47 sts).

**Rows 68 and 69:** Work 2 rows in st-st and cast off 15 sts at beg of these 2 rows (17 sts).

**Row 70:** K2tog, k to last 2 sts k2tog (15 sts).

**Row 71:** Purl.

**Row 72:** K1, m1, k to last st, m1, k1 (17 sts).

**Row 73:** Purl.

**Row 74:** (K1, m1) twice, k to last 2 sts, (m1, k1) twice (21 sts).

**Row 75:** Purl.

**Row 76:** As row 72 (23 sts).

**Rows 77 and 78:** Rep rows 75 and 76 once (25 sts).

**Rows 79 to 91:** Beg with a p row, work 13 rows in st-st.

**Row 92:** K2tog, k to last 2 sts, k2tog (23 sts).

**Row 93:** Purl.

**Rows 94 to 97:** Rep rows 92 and 93, twice more (19 sts).

**Row 98:** (K2tog) twice, k11, (k2tog) twice (15 sts).

**Row 99:** P2tog, p to last 2 sts, p2tog (13 sts).

**Row 100:** (K2tog) twice, k5, (k2tog) twice (9 sts).

Cast off pwise.

# Making up

### Body and head

Place wrong sides of two pieces of
body and head together, matching all
edges. Sew around outside edge using
mattress stitch, leaving a gap in side.
Stuff The Gingerbread Man and sew
up gap.

### Features

Mark position of eyes with two pins on
top half of head with seven clear knitted
stitches in between. Embroider eyes in
black, making a ring of five small chain
stitches around pins for each eye and join
ring with a chain stitch. Embroider nose in
red likewise below eyes and work a second
row of ten chain stitches around first
chain stitches. Embroider mouth in white,
making a smiling row of chain stitches.
Embroider three buttons down body
in black, working as for eyes (see page
171 for how to begin and fasten off the
embroidery invisibly).

Once there was a miller who was so poor that when he died all he could leave
his children was his mill, his donkey and his cat. The eldest son took the mill, the second
son took the donkey and the youngest son, Jack, was left with the cat...

# PUSS IN BOOTS

# Information you'll need

### Finished size
Puss in Boots measures 9½in (24cm) high

### Materials
**Any DK (US: light worsted) yarn**
**Note:** amounts are approximate
10g brown (A)
5g white (B)
10g mustard (C)
15g silver grey (D)
10g blue (E)
5g black (F)
10g claret (G)
5g gold (H)
5g bright red (I)
5g bright green (J)
15g dark green (K)
5g khaki green (L)
Oddments of black and dark grey
for embroidery
1 pair of 3.25mm (UK10:US3) needles
and a spare needle of the same size
Knitters' blunt-ended pins and a needle
for sewing up
Acrylic toy stuffing

### Tension
26 sts x 34 rows measure 4in (10cm)
square over st-st using 3.25mm needles
and DK yarn before stuffing.

### Working instructions
Sew up all row-end seams on right side
using mattress stitch, unless otherwise
stated; a one-stitch seam allowance has
been allowed for this.

# How to make Puss in Boots

## Boots, legs, body and head

### Right boot and leg
Beg at sole of boot, using the thumb method and A, cast on 22 sts.
Place a marker on cast-on edge between the 7th and 8th st of the sts just cast on.
**Row 1 (WS):** Purl.
**Row 2:** K2, (m1, k2) to end (32 sts).

**Rows 3 to 9:** Beg with a p row, work 7 rows in st-st.
**Shape boot**
**Row 10:** K2, (k2tog, k1) 8 times, k6 (24 sts).
**Row 11:** Purl.
**Row 12:** K3, (k2tog) 6 times, k9 (18 sts).
**Rows 13 to 29:** Beg with a p row, work 17 rows in st-st.

Break yarn and set aside.
### Left boot and leg
Beg at sole of boot, using the thumb method and A, cast on 22 sts.
Place a marker on cast-on edge between the 15th and 16th st of the sts just cast on.
**Row 1 (WS):** Purl.
**Row 2:** K2, (m1, k2) to end (32 sts).
**Rows 3 to 9:** Beg with a p row, work 7 rows in st-st.
**Shape boot**
**Row 10:** K7, (k2tog, k1) 8 times, k1 (24 sts).
**Row 11:** Purl.
**Row 12:** K9, (k2tog) 6 times, k3 (18 sts).
**Rows 13 to 29:** Beg with a p row, work 17 rows in st-st.
**Join legs**
**Row 30:** Change to B for lower body and k across sts of left leg, and then with the same yarn cont k across sts of right leg (36 sts).
**Rows 31 to 37:** Beg with a p row, work 7 rows in st-st.
**Rows 38 to 45:** Change to C for upper body and work 8 rows in st-st.
**Shape shoulders**
**Row 46:** K5, (k2tog) 4 times, k10, (k2tog) 4 times, k5 (28 sts).
**Rows 47 to 49:** Beg with a p row, work 3 rows in st-st.
**Rows 50 and 51:** Change to D for head and work 2 rows in st-st.
**Row 52:** K5, (m1, k1) 6 times, k7, (m1, k1) 6 times, k4 (40 sts).
**Rows 53 to 69:** Beg with a p row, work 17 rows in st-st.
**Shape top of head**
**Row 70:** (K2tog, k2) to end (30 sts).
**Row 71 and foll alt row:** Purl.
**Row 72:** (K2tog, k1) to end (20 sts).
**Row 74:** (K2tog) to end (10 sts).
Thread yarn through sts on needle and leave loose.

## Breeches and belt

### First leg

Beg at lower edge, using the thumb method and E, cast on 20 sts.

**Row 1 (WS):** Purl.

**Row 2:** K2, (m1, k4) 4 times, m1, k2 (25 sts).

**Rows 3 to 11:** Beg with a p row, work 9 rows in st-st.

**Rows 12 and 13:** Cast off 2 sts at beg of next 2 rows (21 sts).

Break yarn and set aside.

### Second Leg

Work as first leg but do not break yarn.

### Join legs

**Row 14:** With RS facing, k across sts of second leg, and then with the same yarn cont k across sts of first leg (42 sts).

**Rows 15 to 19:** Beg with a p row, work 5 rows in st-st.

**Rows 20 to 24:** Change to F for belt and work 5 rows in g-st, ending with a RS row. Cast off in g-st.

## Boot tops (make 2)

Using the thumb method and A, cast on 28 sts, WS facing to beg.

**Rows 1 to 9:** Beg with a p row, work 9 rows in st-st.

Cast off.

## Sleeves and paws (make 2)

Beg at sleeve, using the thumb method and C, cast on 6 sts.

**Row 1 (WS):** Purl.

**Row 2:** (K1, m1) twice, k2, (m1, k1) twice (10 sts).

**Row 3:** Purl.

**Row 4:** K1, m1, k to last st, m1, k1 (12 sts).

**Rows 5 to 8:** Rep rows 3 and 4, twice more (16 sts).

Place a marker on first and last st of the last row.

**Rows 9 to 19:** Beg with a p row, work 11 rows in st-st.

**Row 20:** K4, (k2tog, k4) twice (14 sts).

**Rows 21 to 25:** Change to D for paw and beg with a p row, work 5 rows in st-st.

**Row 26:** (K2tog) to end (7 sts).

Thread yarn through sts on needle, pull tight and secure by threading yarn a second time through sts.

## Cuffs (make 2)

Using the thumb method and C, cast on 26 sts and work in g-st.

**Rows 1 and 2:** Work 2 rows in g-st.

**Row 3 (RS):** *K1, (k2tog) twice; rep from * 4 times more, k1 (16 sts).

Cast off in g-st.

## Ear (make 1)

Using the thumb method and D, cast on 16 sts, WS facing to beg.

**Rows 1 to 3:** Beg with a p row, work 3 rows in st-st.

**Row 4:** K2, (k2tog) twice, k4, (k2tog) twice, k2 (12 sts).

**Row 5 and foll alt row:** Purl.

**Row 6:** K1, (k2tog) twice, k2, (k2tog) twice, k1 (8 sts).

**Row 8:** (K2tog) to end (4 sts).

Thread yarn through sts on needle, pull tight and secure by threading yarn a second time through sts.

## Hat

Using the thumb method and G, cast on 60 sts and beg in g-st, RS facing to beg.

**Rows 1 to 8:** Work 8 rows in g-st.

**Row 9:** (K1, k2tog) 4 times, (k2tog) 6 times, (k2tog, k2) 6 times, (k2tog, k1) 4 times (40 sts).

**Rows 10 to 19:** Beg with a k row, work 10 rows in st-st.

**Row 20:** (K2tog, k2) to end (30 sts).

**Row 21 and foll alt row:** Purl.

**Row 22:** (K2tog, k1) to end (20 sts).

**Row 24:** (K2tog) to end (10 sts).

Thread yarn through sts on needle, pull tight and secure by threading yarn a second time through sts.

## Feathers
### (make one in each of H, I and J)

Using the thumb method and H, I or J, cast on 22 sts.

**Row 1 (RS):** K9, (k2tog) twice, k9 (20 sts).

Cast off kwise.

## Tail

Using the thumb method and D, cast on 20 sts, WS facing to beg.

**Rows 1 to 31:** Beg with a p row, work 31 rows in st-st.

**Row 32:** K2tog, k to end (19 sts).

**Rows 33 to 35:** Beg with a p row, work 3 rows in st-st.

**Rows 36 to 47:** Rep rows 32 to 35, 3 times more (16 sts).

**Row 48:** (K2tog) to end (8 sts).

Thread yarn through sts on needle, pull tight and secure by threading yarn a second time through sts.

## Collar of cloak

Using the thumb method and K, cast on 26 sts and work in g-st.

**Row 1 (RS):** Knit.

**Row 2:** K4, (m1, k1) 19 times, k3 (45 sts).

**Row 3:** K38, turn.

**Row 4:** S1k, k30, turn.

**Row 5:** S1k, k25, turn.

**Row 6:** S1k, k20, turn.

**Row 7:** S1k, k to end.

**Row 8:** K3, (m1, k3) to end (59 sts).

Cast off in g-st.

## Cloak

Using the thumb method and K, cast on 35 sts and work in g-st, RS facing to beg.

**Rows 1 to 14:** Work 14 rows in g-st.

**Row 15:** K2, k2tog, k to last 4 sts, k2tog, k2 (33 sts).

**Rows 16 to 20:** Work 5 rows in g-st.

**Row 21:** As row 15 (31 sts).

**Rows 22 to 24:** Work 3 rows in g-st.

**Row 25:** As row 15 (29 sts).

**Row 26:** Knit.

**Rows 27 to 40:** As rows 25 and 26, 7 times more (15 sts).

Cast off in g-st.

## Brooch

Using the thumb method and L, cast on 9 sts.

**Row 1 (WS):** Purl.

Thread yarn through sts on needle, pull tight, secure by threading yarn a second time through sts and oversew row ends.

# Making up

## Boots, legs, body and head

Sew up row ends of ankles of boots and, with markers at tips of toes, oversew cast-on stitches; leg seam will be ½in (13mm) on inside edge of heel. Place a ball of stuffing into toes. Sew up row ends of legs and sew round crotch. Stuff legs and sew up body seam. Stuff body and sew up row ends of head to half way up head. Stuff head, pull stitches on a thread tight at top of head, fasten off and finish sewing up row ends. To shape neck, take a double length of yarn in colour to match upper body and sew a running stitch round last

row of upper body, sewing in and out of every half stitch. Pull tight, knot yarn and sew ends into neck.

## Breeches and belt

Sew up row ends of legs of breeches from lower edge to crotch. Sew round crotch by oversewing and sew up row ends at centre back of breeches and belt. Place breeches on Puss and sew cast-off stitches of belt to first row of upper body using backstitch all the way round.

## Boot tops

Fold boot tops and oversew cast-on and cast-off stitches. Place boot tops round top of boots and sew up row ends and sew lower edge of boot tops to top of boots.

## Sleeves and paws

Sew up row ends of paws and place a small ball of stuffing into paws. Sew up sleeves from wrists to markers at underarm. Stuff sleeves and leave armholes open. Sew arms to Puss at either side, sewing cast-on stitches at top of arms to row below neck.

## Cuffs

Place cuffs around wrists and sew up row ends. Sew cuffs to wrists using back stitch all the way round.

## Features

Embroider features in black and mark position of eyes with two pins on 11th row above neck with four clear knitted stitches in between. Work a vertical chain stitch for each eye and a second chain stitch on top of first chain stitch. Embroider nose on second row below eyes taking three horizontal stitches close together over two stitches. Using picture

as a guide, embroider mouth and whiskers using straight stitches. Embroider a buckle on belt in dark grey using double straight stitches (see page 171 for how to begin and fasten off the embroidery invisibly).

## Hat, feathers and ear

Sew up row ends of hat and oversew row ends of brim. Sew up row ends of ear with seam at centre back. Lightly stuff top of hat and with seam at right hand side, pin hat to right side of head and ear to left side, and sew hat and ear to head using back stitch for hat on right side of base of brim, sewing through hat to head. Fold cast-off stitches of feathers in half and oversew. Using picture as a guide, sew feathers to hat, turn up brim and sew in place.

## Tail

Roll tail up from shaped row ends to long edge and sew long edge in place. Sew end of tail to Puss at back, sewing through breeches to body.

## Cloak collar, cloak and brooch

Place cloak collar around neck and join beneath chin. Sew cast-on stitches of collar to neck. Sew cast-off stitches of cloak to back of neck beneath collar. Sew brooch to centre front of collar beneath chin.

# FEE-FI-FO-FUM...

Who's been eating my porridge?

YOU SHALL GO TO THE BALL!

# Techniques

... and they all lived happily ever after.

# Getting started

## Buying yarn

All the patterns in this book are worked in double knitting yarn (DK yarn; known as light worsted in the US). There are many DK yarns on the market, from natural fibres to acrylic blends. Acrylic is a good choice, as it washes without shrinking, although you should always follow the care instructions on the ball band. Be cautious about using a brushed or mohair-type yarn if the toy is intended for a baby or a very young child, as the fluffy fibres could be swallowed.

## Tension

Tension is not critical when knitting toys if the correct yarn and needles are used. All the toys in this book are knitted on 3.25mm (UK10:US3) knitting needles. This should turn out at approximately 26 stitches and 34 rows over 4in (10cm) square.

## Safety advice

Some of the toys have small pieces and trimmings, which could present a choking hazard. Make sure that small parts are sewn down securely before giving any of the toys to a baby or young child.

# Slip knot

1  Leave a long length of yarn: as a rough guide, allow ⅜in (1cm) for each stitch to be cast on, plus an extra length for sewing up. Wind the yarn from the ball round your left index finger from front to back and then to front again. Slide the loop from your finger and pull the new loop through from the centre. Place this loop from back to front on to the needle that is in your right hand.

2  Pull the tail of yarn down to tighten the knot slightly and pull the yarn from the ball to form a loose knot.

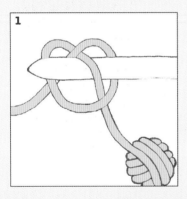

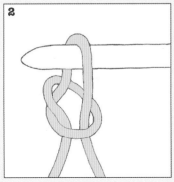

# Casting on

## Thumb method

1  Make a slip knot. Hold the needle in your right hand with your index finger on the slip knot loop to keep it in place.

2  Wrap the loose tail end round your left thumb, from front to back. Push the needle's point through the thumb loop from front to back. Wind the ball end of the yarn round the needle from left to right.

3  Pull the loop through the thumb loop, then remove your thumb. Gently pull the new loop tight using the tail yarn.

Repeat this process until the required number of stitches are on the needle.

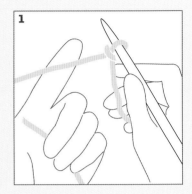

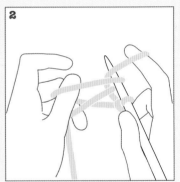

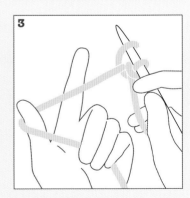

# Knit stitch

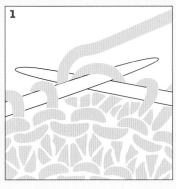

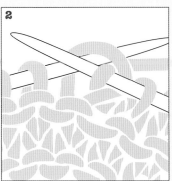

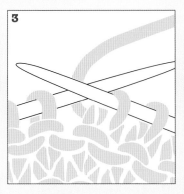

**1** Hold needle with stitches in left hand. Hold yarn at back of work and insert point of right-hand empty needle into the front loop of the first stitch. Wrap yarn around point of right-hand needle in a clockwise direction using your index finger.

**2** With yarn still wrapped around the point, bring the right-hand needle back towards you through the loop of the first stitch. Try to keep the free yarn fairly taut but not too slack or tight.

**3** With the new stitch firmly on the right-hand needle, gently pull the old stitch to the right and off the tip of the left-hand needle. Repeat for all the knit stitches across the row.

# Purl stitch

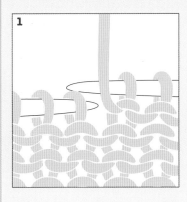

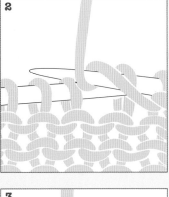

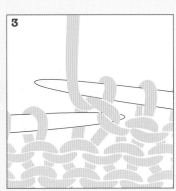

**1** Hold needles with stitches in left hand and hold yarn at front of work.

**2** Insert point of right-hand empty needle into the front loop of the first stitch. Wrap yarn around point of right-hand needle in an anti-clockwise direction using index finger.

**3** With yarn still wrapped around point of right-hand needle, bring it back through the stitch. Try to keep free yarn taut but not too slack or tight. With the new stitch firmly on the right-hand needle, gently pull the old stitch off the tip of the left-hand needle. Repeat for all the purl stitches along the row.

# Types of stitch

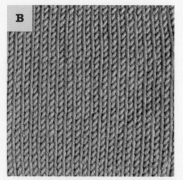

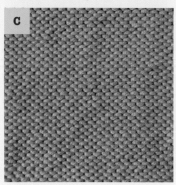

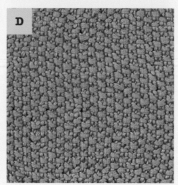

## Moss stitch (D)

This stitch creates a bumpy-looking fabric made by alternating purl and knit stitches in a row. To create moss stitch, you need an odd number of stitches on the needle.

1 With the yarn at the back of the work, knit the first stitch in the normal way.

2 Bring the yarn through the two needles to the front of your work.

3 With the yarn now at the front, purl the stitch.

4 Next you need to knit a stitch, so take the yarn back between the needles and knit a stitch. Continue to k1, (p1, k1) to the end of the row. This row is repeated.

## Garter stitch (A)

This is made by knitting every row.

## Stocking stitch (B)

Probably the most commonly used stitch in knitting, this is created by knitting on the right side and purling on the wrong side.

## Reverse stocking stitch (C)

This is made by purling on the right side and knitting on the wrong side.

# Increasing

Three methods are used in this book for increasing the number of stitches: m1, kfb and pfb.

**M1** Make a stitch by picking up the horizontal loop between the needles from front to back and placing it onto the left-hand needle. Now knit into the back of it to twist it, or purl into the back of it on a purl row.

**Kfb** Make a stitch on a knit row by knitting into the front then back of the next stitch. To do this, simply knit into the next stitch but do not slip it off. Take the point of the right-hand needle around and knit again into the back of the stitch before removing the loop from the left-hand needle. You now have made two stitches out of one.

**Pfb** Make a stitch on a purl row by purling into the front then back of the next stitch. To do this, purl the next stitch but do not slip it off the needle. Take the point of the right-hand needle around and purl again into the back of the stitch before removing the loop from the left-hand needle. You now have made two stitches out of one.

# Decreasing

To decrease a stitch, simply knit two stitches together to make one stitch out of the two stitches, or if the instructions say k3tog, then knit three stitches together to make one out of the three stitches. To achieve a neat appearance to your finished work, this is done as follows:

At the beginning of a knit row and throughout the row, k2tog by knitting two stitches together through the front of the loops.

At the end of a knit row, if these are the very last two stitches in the row, then knit together through the back of the loops.

At the beginning of a purl row, if these are the very first stitches in the row, then purl together through the back of the loops. Purl two together along the rest of the row through the front of the loops.

# Casting off

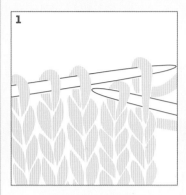

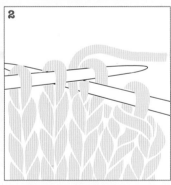

**1** Knit two stitches onto the right-hand needle, then slip the first stitch over the second and let it drop off the needle. One stitch remains.

**2** Knit another stitch so you have two stitches on the right-hand needle again.

Repeat the process until only one stitch is left on the left-hand needle. Break the yarn and thread it through the remaining stitch.

# Threading yarn through stitches

Sometimes you will see 'thread yarn through stitches on needle, pull tight and secure'. To do this, first break the yarn, leaving a long end, and thread a needle with this end.

Pass the needle through all the stitches on the knitting needle, slipping each stitch off the knitting needle in turn. Draw the yarn through the stitches.

To secure, pass the needle once again through all the stitches in a complete circle and pull tight.

# Placing a marker

When placing a marker on the cast-on edge, thread a needle with yarn in a contrasting colour and count the number of stitches to where the marker is to be placed. Pass the needle between these stitches, tie a loose loop around the cast-on edge with a double knot and trim the ends. To place a marker on a stitch, thread a needle with contrast yarn and pass this needle through the stitch on the knitting needle to be marked. Tie a loose loop with a double knot and trim the ends.

# Sewing up

The characters in this book are put together using simple sewing techniques.

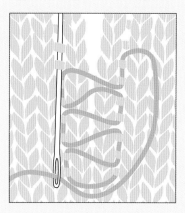

### Mattress stitch
Sew up all row ends using mattress stitch, one stitch in from edge by taking small straight stitches back and forth on the right side of work (see illustration). A one-stitch seam allowance has been allowed for this.

### Back stitch
For sewing on hats, hair and belts, sew on the right side of one layer to the layer underneath, and bring the needle out at the beginning of the stitch line, make a straight stitch and bring the needle out slightly further along the stitch line. Insert the needle at the end of the first stitch and bring it out still further along the stitch line. Continue in the same way to create a line of joined stitches.

### Running stitch
The necks of the dolls are shaped with a running stitch. Take a double length of yarn and thread a needle and take the needle in and out of every half stitch to create a line of gathering stitches around the neck. Do not secure either end of the yarn but pull both ends tight and knot yarn with a double knot. Then sew ends into neck.

# Finishing touches

## Embroidery

To begin embroidery invisibly, tie a knot in the end of the yarn. Take a large stitch through the work, coming up to begin the embroidery. Allow the knot to disappear through the knitting and be caught in the stuffing. To fasten off invisibly, sew a few stitches back and forth through the work, inserting the needle where the yarn comes out.

## Straight stitch

Come up to start the embroidery at one end of the stitch then go back down at the end of the stitch, coming up in a different place to start the next stitch.

## Chain stitch

Bring the needle up through your work to start the first stitch and hold down the thread with the left thumb. Insert the needle in the same place and bring the point out a short distance away. Keeping the working thread under the needle point, pull the loop of thread to form a chain.

## Stem stitch

Starting at the left-hand side and working towards the right-hand side, work small stitches backwards along the stitch line with the thread always emerging on the left-hand side of the previous stitch.

## Making a twisted cord

A twisted cord is used for the giant (page 56) and the cow's tail (page 47).

1   Cut even strands of yarn to the number and length stated in the pattern and knot each end. Anchor one end – you could tie it to a door handle or a chair, or ask a friend to hold it.

2   Take the other end and twist until it is tightly wound.

3   Hold the centre of the cord, and place the two ends together. Release the centre, so the two halves twist together. Smooth it out and knot the ends together.

## Stuffing and aftercare

Spend a little time stuffing your knitted figure evenly. Acrylic toy stuffing is ideal; use plenty, but not so much that it stretches the knitted fabric so the stuffing can be seen through the stitches. Fill out any base, keeping it flat so the figure will be able to stand upright. Tweezers are useful for stuffing small parts.

Washable filling is recommended for all the stuffed figures so that you can hand-wash them with a non-biological detergent. Do not spin or tumble dry, but gently squeeze the excess water out, arrange the figure into its original shape, and leave it to dry.

# Abbreviations

| | |
|---|---|
| **alt** | alternate |
| **beg** | beginning |
| **cont** | continue |
| **dec** | decrease/decreasing |
| **DK** | double knitting |
| **foll** | following |
| **g-st** | garter stitch: knit every row |
| **inc** | increase/increasing |
| **k** | knit |
| **k2tog** | knit two stitches together: if these are the very last in the row, then work together through back of loops |
| **k3tog** | knit three stitches together |
| **kfb** | make two stitches out of one: knit into the front then the back of the next stitch |
| **kwise** | knitwise |
| **LH** | left hand |
| **m1** | make one stitch: pick up horizontal loop between the needles from front to back and work into the back of it to twist it |
| **moss-st** | moss stitch: knit 1 stitch, (purl next stitch, knit next stitch) to end |
| **patt** | pattern |
| **p** | purl |
| **p2tog** | purl two stitches together: if these stitches are the very first in the row, then work together through back of loops |
| **p3tog** | purl three stitches together |
| **pfb** | make two stitches out of one: purl into the front then the back of the next stitch |

| | |
|---|---|
| **pwise** | purlwise |
| **rem** | remaining |
| **rep** | repeat(ed) |
| **rev st-st** | reverse stocking stitch: purl on the right side, knit on the wrong side |
| **RH** | right hand |
| **RS** | right side |
| **slk** | slip one stitch knit ways |
| **slp** | slip one stitch purl ways |
| **st(s)** | stitch(es) |
| **st-st** | stocking stitch: knit on the right side, purl on the wrong side |
| **tbl** | through back of loop(s) |
| **tog** | together |
| **WS** | wrong side |
| **yf** | yarn forward |
| **yb** | yarn back |
| **( )** | repeat instructions between brackets as many times as instructed |
| **\*** | repeat from \* as instructed |

# Conversions

## Knitting needles

| UK | US | Metric |
|----|----|--------|
| 8  | 6  | 4mm    |
| 10 | 3  | 3.25mm |

## Terms

| UK | US |
|----|----|
| Cast off | Bind off |
| Moss stitch | Seed stitch |
| Stocking stitch | Stockinette stitch |
| Tension | Gauge |
| Yarn forward | Yarn over |

## Yarn weight

| UK | US |
|----|----|
| Double knitting | Light worsted |

# About the author

Sarah Keen is passionate about knitting, finding it relaxing and therapeutic. She discovered her love of the craft at a very early age; her mother taught her to knit when she was just four years old and by the age of nine she was making jackets and jumpers.

Sarah now works as a freelance pattern designer and finds calculating rows and stitches challenging but fascinating. She is experienced in designing knitted toys for children, and also enjoys writing patterns for charity. This is her fifth book for GMC Publications; she is also the author of *Knitted Nursery Rhymes*, *Knitted Wild Animals*, *Knitted Farm Animals* and *Knitted Noah's Ark*.

# Acknowledgements

The author would like to thank all family and friends who have enquired and enthused about the book at all stages of its coming together.

Special thanks to Cynthia of Clare Wools (www.clarewools.co.uk) for stocking the lovely Sirdar Bonus DK yarn, and thanks to all the team at GMC.

GMC would like to thank Amelia and Isabella Holmwood and Emma Foster for their help with the styling.

# Index

To place an order, or to request a catalogue, contact:
**GMC Publications Ltd**
Castle Place, 166 High Street, Lewes, East Sussex, BN7 1XU
United Kingdom
Tel: +44 (0)1273 488005
www.gmcbooks.com